THE CRACKS THAT
LET THE LIGHT IN

THE CRACKS THAT LET THE LIGHT IN

What I learned from my disabled son

JESSICA MOXHAM

ENDEAVOUR

First published in Great Britain in 2021 by Endeavour,
an imprint of Octopus Publishing Group Ltd
Carmelite House
50 Victoria Embankment
London EC4Y 0DZ
www.octopusbooks.co.uk

An Hachette UK Company
www.hachette.co.uk

ISBN 978-1-91306-834-9

A CIP catalogue record for this book is available from
the British Library.

Printed and bound in the United Kingdom

1 3 5 7 9 10 8 6 4 2

This FSC® label means that materials used for the product
have been responsibly sourced

For James, without whom there
wouldn't be these children,
and it would all be less fun.

CONTENTS

NOTE

Some names and identifying details of people have been changed to protect their privacy. I use pseudonyms for my children.

The way I talk about my son, Ben, has changed as he has got older. Language surrounding disability is something I explore in the book and I have learned a lot about it since Ben was born. There are reasons – linguistic, personal and political – that people prefer certain terms. I talk about Ben being disabled because this encompasses the ways in which he interacts with, and is seen by, the world. The word 'disabled' is not a slur, it is a carefully chosen identity. People with impairments should be able to choose how they are described; for now, I am using this description for my son.

PREFACE

We corral our kids, Ben, Max and Molly, aged nine, six and three, into the car on a Sunday morning before 10am to drive north over the river to Tate Britain, where we know we can park right by the entrance. It is January 2019 and bright but cold. As we unload ourselves from the car, a couple walk past with a buggy and stop near a tree. The mother unpacks a potty and sets it up on the pavement for her son to use. He is probably younger than Molly and, while I push her arms into her coat and try to locate her hat on the floor of the car as she asks me about slugs, I think again that we need to toilet train her.

We race down the side of the building, my husband James running with Ben's wheelchair to the accessible entrance, get out of the cold and begin the process of removing the coats we had only just put on each child.

There is an exhibition of Turner Prize nominees and I ask a man at the front desk whether it is suitable for children. 'I don't think there's any nudity or sex,' he says. I don't mind about nudity, but I am nervous of what the naked people might be doing since I had wheeled Ben into an inappropriate Gilbert & George exhibition a few years previously.

And he is right, no sex. The pieces are all video works. One of the films is about identity and belonging with sweeping footage of ancient standing stones on remote islands in Scotland. The other visitors are sitting quietly and I can see Ben is engrossed. The only noises are the squawks of island birds and the rhythmical clicks of Ben's tongue.

Ben's muscles move involuntarily, all the time, including those in his mouth. His tongue moves a lot, though not in a way that can manage food. It means Ben can't eat, he dribbles and he makes a clicking noise sometimes. When he was first at nursery, the staff would call him Dolphin Boy, as if he were trying to communicate on some level unintelligible to mere humans. He would make the sound when he was relaxed or interested, never when he was tense or bored. We would often respond with our own clicks like we were speaking a secret language. I liked them and I think Ben did too. Over the years he has clicked less and I miss it. James and I sometimes talk with nostalgia about the clicks, wondering what had changed in his tongue, mouth or brain over the years to make them more rare.

When Ben was younger, I was self-conscious about him being noisy, particularly in very quiet places. For a child who doesn't talk, Ben can be quite loud: there are kicks which make his wheelchair squeak, whinging noises to complain, shrieks if he is excited and the clicks. In silent galleries, planetariums or theatres the noises can jar. I'm the kind of person who would rather not eat sweets than risk the noise of a crackling packet in a cinema. But Ben loves the cinema so we take him anyway, despite the noise. Now he is almost ten, I hardly notice the sounds because I am so used to them. I am less likely to see whether other people have noticed and I care less about what anyone thinks.

After the videos, we wander through the main galleries of historical paintings. Somewhere around the seventeenth century, Molly takes off her shoes and tries to jump off an elegant wooden bench in the centre of the room before shouting, 'I want to run!' I try to tame her, to avoid her rushing into a room filled with carefully calibrated metronomes and knocking them all off course. Molly has just turned three and is extremely enthusiastic. I hear James occasionally asking Max not to lean too close to the paintings and I glimpse him leaning on Ben's wheelchair instead. Max is six and more contained than Molly – less supervision required, his emotions and impulses not quite as close to the surface.

As we walk around the Tate with our children we aren't once self-conscious about Ben and his behaviour. We are, however, mindful of his small whirlwind of a sister who risks careering into art of national importance. When Ben was a baby, I would have struggled to imagine that we could have mornings like this, in an art gallery, with three children in tow, and Ben the least of our worries.

1

I had been in labour for many hours when I am told my baby Ben is in distress and needs to be born immediately. His heart rate is low, they say, and there is no time for local anaesthetic.

There is a sharp pain and out he comes. He is immediately cut from me and carried over to a plinth where midwives lean over him, suctioning and murmuring. There is silence apart from low, urgent conversation between midwives and then doctors. People hurry in and out and pay my baby close attention. Where there should be the sound of a baby crying there is nothing.

I know very little about the realities of childbirth but I know a baby is meant to make some noise. Something has gone horribly wrong. After hours of gas and air and contractions I feel detached while also very present in a body that is tired and hurt.

I have a thought that is sharp and brittle: this might not be OK.

'He's not making any noise,' I say to James.

I haven't yet seen Ben when he is taken away to intensive care in a flurry of medics. I am told he had been born unresponsive but has been resuscitated. He now needs specialist help. It is serious. James steps out of the room to call my parents.

After my mum and dad arrive, a doctor comes in and stands at the end of my bed while James holds my hand. 'I think that at some point during your labour your baby didn't get enough oxygen. He is now very sick,' she says.

I ask to visit Ben and, since I can't yet walk, my bed is pushed along bright corridors and through doors to the neonatal unit nearby. It doesn't feel right to be travelling through the public areas of the hospital, passing the relatives of other labouring women, in the bed I have just given birth in. I check I am fully covered with a sheet.

Two midwives squeeze my bed into the room where my baby is lying on a cot, very still, plump, not yet clean and covered in tubes. I am not allowed to touch him. I don't know what to think.

I have still not delivered the placenta so, after returning from seeing Ben, I am taken to an operating theatre to have it removed. As the doctor finishes the procedure and I am being stitched, the anaesthetist speaks to me kindly, holding my hand, and I realize that I am a person who should be treated sympathetically.

I arrive in the recovery room and am told that my baby needs to be transferred to a different hospital with expertise in a particular cooling treatment that this hospital doesn't have.

This cooling treatment may help minimize the damage caused by oxygen deprivation.

'Can I see him before he leaves?' I ask.

'I'll see what I can do,' the neonatologist replies. 'I'll speak to the transfer team.'

Ben arrives a while later in a different cot to the one I had last seen him in, surrounded by machines and tubes, pushed by a team of four people who will keep him alive for this journey. Their uniforms look professional and urgent. I can only just see Ben through the medical equipment surrounding him. They manage to manoeuvre his cot close enough so that when they open a small window in the side, I can hold his tiny hand for the first time. I didn't know that this was how a birth could go. I don't feel prepared for any of it.

Later, in a private room, I will my legs to recover from anaesthetic as James sleeps on a hard sofa nearby. When healthcare assistants come to check me, they don't seem to realize how ill my baby is or that he has been taken away to another hospital. 'I need to leave,' I say. 'I have to get to my baby.'

I am consumed by a determination to go home because then I can go to Ben. My mother- and father-in-law have already gone to the new hospital and tell us he has arrived safely but I hate the thought of him being alone. When I can feel my legs again, I carefully lower myself off the bed and walk slowly to the loo. 'I have done a wee,' I say to the midwife who comes when I press the buzzer next to my bed, this being necessary to be discharged. 'Can I leave now?' I don't know how Ben is, or really what he looks like, and I need to be closer to him.

Once I am allowed to leave the hospital, my parents come
to collect us. When we arrive at their house, Dad offers us roast
chicken in front of the fire but I am so tired I can barely eat. I
walk slowly upstairs and sleep deeply. The next morning, my
mum drives me and James across London, putting a cushion
on the passenger seat for me and trying to drive over the
bumps as slowly as she can.

Ben is sedated and covered in sensors and wires. We can't
hold him. All we can do is stroke the exposed areas of his skin
and listen to the warning tones of monitors nearby while he
remains silent and still. I stare at his face, imprinting his features
on my memory. I have never been in an intensive care unit
before. I am shocked to find myself here, grateful to hold my
baby's hand but overwhelmed by the surroundings and his
apparent delicacy.

For the next week, we visit each day to spend time with
Ben. The immediate daily tasks feel onerous in my injured
body. It takes concentration to get dressed, travel to the hospital,
remember to eat, take painkillers, decode the monitors above
Ben's head. We begin learning the language of critical illness
but I refuse to fully engage. James has conversations with
doctors about Ben's prognosis and translates parts for me. I just
make sure I can turn up, hold Ben's hand, painstakingly collect
my colostrum – my first breastmilk – in miniature quantities
and hand them over to the intensive care nurses.

James says he is going to arrange an appointment for us
to register the birth and when I overhear his conversation
on the phone I realize a doctor has told him it should be

done urgently. I know that there is often a long wait to get an appointment but James gets one quickly because, I gather, there is a risk Ben could die before we've had a chance to register that he has lived. James and I don't talk about this with each other.

Three days after Ben's birth, some of the wires and tubes can be removed and his breathing support reduced. After two more days, we can hold Ben briefly. James and I squeeze next to each other on an armchair with a pillow on our laps. A nurse carefully arranges the tubes and wires to one side and picks Ben up. She lowers him onto the pillow and I cradle him, unable to really feel the weight or shape of him through the pillow but grateful to be this close. James has one arm around me and the other around Ben's legs and we sit gazing at this wondrous child who we can just about feel and see among the paraphernalia keeping him alive.

As Ben nears a week old, it becomes more likely he will live. His breathing support is reduced again and some more of the monitoring wires are removed. We can hold him without a pillow and see his face. He has survived and I am so thankful – that he is alive, that I can cuddle him and that I don't have to monitor every breath in case the next one doesn't come.

We are taken into a small room to discuss the results of a scan of Ben's brain. A doctor quietly talks us through the events of the last five days and explains the likely impact of an 'insult' like Ben's, when the brain has been cut off from the oxygen it needs. We all face a computer screen and, as she clicks the mouse, we can see black-and-white images of our son's brain, metaphorical slices through skull and tissue.

The doctor explains what we are looking at and even our unskilled eyes can see that areas that should be dense are murky. She talks to us about the possibility that Ben's brain might not communicate with the muscles that control his body. The messages might not get through, or might speak in the wrong dialect. Ben's brain will likely speak a language that his arms, legs, hands and tongue cannot understand.

I am relieved that my baby has survived but devastated that he is injured. Afterwards, we pace the streets surrounding the hospital, me crying and James holding my hand. I am distraught.

As Ben's health improves he is moved to a different room within the ward with less beeping, fewer nurses and more light. Our families join us at the hospital each day. I want to be with Ben all the time, holding him, feeling the undeniable weight of him. If James or I are not with Ben then I want to know someone else is. I don't want him to be alone.

One evening, when he only has two wires or tubes attached, I am cuddling Ben when a nurse says, 'Careful! If you hold him all the time he'll get used to it and you won't be able to put him down!' That's exactly what I want, I think to myself. I wasn't able to hold him at all until two days ago and I am worried he doesn't know who I am. He hasn't yet made a single noise. All I want is for him to realize I am his mother, want to be close to me, and be able to cry if he's not.

When James and I leave the hospital after visiting Ben we bump into a friend. 'When are you due?' she asks as she looks down at my swollen belly. 'He's been born,' I say. 'He's ill in hospital.' She is aghast. 'I'm sorry. I had no idea.' I try to make her feel better before we go to buy a sandwich. I haven't spoken to anyone outside of my family. I have left social media and I don't check my email. I don't want to talk to anyone I don't have to. James fields messages and calls, and in the first month I will only see a few friends who have arranged to visit.

We are told Ben will be transferred to our local hospital when he is a week old but it is not clear exactly when this will happen. James calls the hospital just before we leave home one morning to check how Ben is. 'He's not here,' they say. 'He's been transferred. Did no one tell you?'

I feel redundant. My son was crossing the Thames in an ambulance with strangers and I didn't even know. I don't know what makes a mother, but I am certain I don't yet qualify.

We can now walk to the hospital each day. As I heal, I am able to walk faster and James doesn't need to support me as much, though we still walk close, arms linked or hands held. It snows and we change from wellies to indoor shoes by the lockers in the neonatal unit before we go in to see Ben. Compared with tiny premature babies, he looks solid and substantial but when we hold him he is small and floppy.

We hold Ben as much as possible. One night we leave my younger sister Maddy holding him while we go for dinner. When we return Ben is back in his cot and she is apologetic.

'I cuddled him for an hour,' she says, 'until I couldn't feel my hands any more. I was too scared to move but then a nurse came and helped me put him back.'

Just before Christmas we are taken into a small room with a neurologist, Dr M. I notice a box of tissues on the desk. The room has medical textbooks on the shelves and I wonder what happens in here when it's not being used to deliver bad news. Dr M has examined Ben's body and seen the scan of his brain which he confirms is insubstantial in places where it should be robust. He is gentle but factual, delivering bad news as kindly as he can. 'It isn't certain,' he says among other caveats, 'but it is likely he will have cerebral palsy.'

We are told Ben's physical movements will be affected, the most pertinent of which in that first month is his ability to control his tongue and swallow. A more junior doctor sits next to Dr M and says nothing but looks grave. Later I will marvel at how Dr M managed to deliver this uncompromising news to us in a way that didn't make me hate him, like I did with other medics in those early months who told me news I didn't want to hear. Dr M made me feel he could be our light in an otherwise gloomy tunnel – Ben's condition was serious, but he would do all he could to help us and all hope was not lost.

Ben's most urgent problem is his difficulty with feeding. I was trying to breastfeed him every day and though I didn't know how it was meant to feel, the slackness of Ben's mouth didn't seem right. James and I were also offering him a bottle, but he swallowed very little milk. I am so preoccupied with these tasks – breastfeeding, bottle feeding, expressing milk to a three-hour schedule – that there is barely time to think. However, Ben is getting almost all of his nutrition through a nasogastric (NG) tube. As he approaches a month old he is doing well – he now makes little noises and cries when distressed, his breathing is reliable, his oxygen saturation good, his organs stable – but it is his inability to drink that is keeping him in hospital.

Our only hope of leaving, which we are desperate to do, is to give Ben milk through his feeding tube and so James and I are formally trained. Forms are filled in and competencies checked. I want to be able to be Ben's mother rather than feeling like I am one person in a team who cares for him, and often the least important member. I want to be able to give him a bath, rather than watch someone else do it. I want him to realize I am the most important one. I don't wear perfume in the hope that he will learn my smell, or earrings so I can nestle him into my neck unscratched. When Ben is five weeks old, we are allowed to take him home, to look after him unsupervised.

But there is another problem. Our home, with our books, pictures and cats, is thousands of miles away in Qatar where James had been working as a diplomat in the British Embassy and I have a job as an architect. For the last three years we have been living in the Middle East – in Damascus in Syria and then Doha in Qatar. We were meant to be having a baby in London and then returning there but that now feels unlikely. So we live in my childhood home with my mum and dad.

James has to travel back periodically to his job in Qatar. My dad is a doctor which is reassuring and my mum is excellent in a crisis so she helps with everything, but I can barely keep up with the schedule of keeping Ben nourished. They are helping me constantly, and yet it is still a punishing regime.

We are feeding Ben through his tube and with a bottle through the day and night. When we aren't feeding, we are washing and sterilizing the syringes, bottles and pumping equipment. I'm too busy keeping my baby alive to have the time or space to enjoy him. I stop expressing milk because it feels like that is the one thing that isn't absolutely essential. When I answer the door to the postman bearing gifts from friends and cards of congratulation from around the world, I barely register them before I move on to my next task.

The feeding tube should stay in place, stuck to his cheek with a rectangle of plaster, for one month before being removed and a new one inserted down the other side of Ben's nose. But Ben's skin is sensitive so the adhesive dressing often comes away, or he grabs the end of the tube accidentally and it is pulled free. Occasionally he sneezes it out. Late one night, one week after bringing Ben home, I feel in Ben's wicker crib for the end of the tube and come across the entire tube buried under his body. I knew this could happen but I am still shocked. It needs to be put back before I can feed him so I quietly wake James and we pack Ben into his car seat, taking a new tube and an explanatory letter to A&E. We tell the nurses what has happened and they put the tube back down within half an hour. When we return to the house my parents are still asleep. I am thankful we live so close to a hospital and that it has been such a simple procedure, but I wonder how many more times we will have to do this trip. Is this what we do now – take our baby to hospital in the middle of the night so we can feed him?

To avoid this I learn how to put the feeding tube in myself so that we won't have to go to hospital every time it comes out. There is nothing nice to be said about pushing a small, stiff but flexible tube into your son's nose, past the resistance of the back of his throat and down his oesophagus. Ben waves his arms furiously while I'm trying to get to his face so he has to be swaddled and held down as he bucks in protest. Once the tube is in, someone has to hold it still on his cheek while I check it's in the right place by pulling back some fluid from his stomach and checking the pH, and then I attach pieces of pristine adhesive to his face and remove the guide wire from the tube.

I know some parents don't do this. They don't want to be their child's nurse when there are nurses that can do it. I want to do as much for him as I can, and if this is what it takes to ensure he is fed, I will do it. I thought I would nourish him with breastmilk but instead I must ensure he can be fed through a tube so I take that on fully, wholeheartedly. I hate putting the tubes down, but I want to be able to feed him. I want to be everything to him. I realize I will do anything for him.

In between the tube changes we change the dressing, which means pulling the old one off his cheek. This hurts and he lets me know it. Once, we left the tube on one cheek for a full month because we were so grateful that we hadn't had to change it but then the skin on his plump cheek took almost three months to recover. Ben will scream while I am adjusting or inserting the tube – he knows what's coming as soon as he's held down – but will then calm quickly once it's finished and he's cuddled. I can't decide whether it's awful that he has learned to anticipate something so unpleasant or good that he recovers quickly. I hope that I am cuddling him enough to counteract the discomfort.

His delicate, newborn skin means his cheeks are constantly sore. When I see other babies, I am taken aback by their smooth cheeks, by the fact that they've never had to have great wads of adhesive messing up their faces. When the tube falls out one evening, I give Ben a bath and remove the plaster. His cheeks are not too red and for a few hours I have an unadorned baby. He has pale skin – so pale that anxious medics sometimes ask us whether he is always this colour – and reminds me of an angelic cherub in a painting. I take a photo and it is the first photo I have of his face with nothing on it. When James gets back from work we spend a little while with our sweet baby before James wraps him in a towel and holds him down and I push another tube up his nose against his will.

One morning the tube falls out when James is at work and my parents are away. I phone a family friend who can walk to my house in ten minutes. She has never seen this done before but I trust that she is practical enough to be able to assist me without being overwhelmed. By the time she arrives I have prepared everything I need on our dining table and found a large, stretchy sheet. I wrap the sheet round and round Ben so only his head is sticking out. I tell my friend she will need to hold him more tightly than she imagines. As I begin Ben starts crying and I hope his tears won't stop the adhesive sticking. It is a strange thing to ask someone to come and help you make your child cry and I am grateful for her stoicism.

The constant process of sticking, unpeeling, pushing and pulling is always done by me. I have to purposely cause pain to my baby in order to make sure he can be kept hydrated; filled up with milk like he's a car at the garage and therefore maintain those podgy cheeks and rolls of fat on his forearms. It is the only way to keep him alive so I feel I have no choice. James is not always there because of work; he doesn't offer to learn to do it and it doesn't occur to me to be resentful because I want to be needed. Of all the ways that motherhood is not what I imagined, the dependency is what I expected. James shares everything else – feeding, changing, comforting – but this bit is mine and, to me, it proves how devoted I am.

People are surprised by my no-nonsense willingness to get on with it. I put Ben's tube down when we have to make another trip to A&E rather than letting a nurse or a doctor do it. I pull the tube back a couple of centimetres in the middle of an X-ray room when they need to fill his stomach with Barium to check whether he has reflux. I put down three tubes in twenty-four hours when he coughs the first up into his mouth and tears the second off his cheek after a night of crying. All the time we are reminded of the danger – the possibility of the tube moving, going down into his lungs and them filling with milk. We live with a permanent backdrop of peril: the tube might come out and we won't be able to feed him; the tube might go down into his trachea and we will drown his lungs.

When we hold Ben he buries his face in our chests and rubs it from side to side. He can't get his hands to his face otherwise and I think this is him seeking comfort, itching the plaster on his cheek and enjoying the pressure. It feels good to him and leaves us with snotty swipes on the front of our jumpers. But I am constantly on edge, wondering if the nuzzling will dislodge the tube. I hate that the thing that he enjoys doing, that soothes him, is something that makes me anxious.

Keeping Ben fed requires a certain toughness of mothering. It is in the same territory as forcing children to take horrible medicine but it feels far more harsh and relentless. I have to be both nurturing and brutal. I hope that, surrounded by kissing and singing, cuddling and smiling, Ben remembers the good times and the horror will fade. Mothering, it would seem, isn't about making your child happy all the time. Sometimes it's about making your child cry because there is no alternative and hoping that he will forgive you.

One morning in the days after Ben was born, I had been in the kitchen with my mum. Ben was still in hospital. 'I just want to check,' my mum said, 'that you know none of this is your fault. You couldn't have done anything differently. You didn't do anything wrong.' I did know, though it didn't make me any less sad, and I cried, again.

I just don't understand how I have ended up in a situation where I'm feeding my baby by holding a syringe of milk above his head, attached to a feeding tube. I did birth preparation classes and they told me about the benefits of natural childbirth and breastfeeding. I had no idea there was a shadow world where you aren't sure your baby will live, then you don't know how to feed them, and every aspect of their life is unclear. I just don't know if everything is going to be OK.

2

The week that Ben left hospital I bought a portable rocking chair for him and a book for me – *Life After Birth* by Kate Figes. It's difficult to fit reading into the relentlessness of our days (I don't touch a novel that a friend gives me as a birthing gift) but in *Life After Birth* I find pages that resonate. 'If you feel that you have lost control over your life, you probably have, but you are not alone, and as the baby gets older life will slip into a new pattern. If you find it hard looking after your baby… remember that motherhood is an acquired skill, that you are entitled to an apprenticeship and that no one expects you to turn professional overnight.'

But I did need to be professional. I needed to be a nurse to my baby and I had categorically lost control over my life. The problem was that while others expected their lives to slip into a new pattern, I had no idea what the future held. I had been apprehensive about motherhood but now I felt totally lost. None of what I was doing matched up with what I had been told it would be like, or how I heard others describe it. I wasn't so much upset that Ben was different to other children, but more disorientated that I wasn't sure what to hold onto.

After having worried that Ben made no noise, I now find him loud. Within a week of getting home from hospital, Ben started getting upset and squirmy while we were feeding him. Feeding isn't a comforting, pleasurable thing for him. He has gastro-oesophageal reflux and a cow's milk protein allergy and it means that rather than milk calmly flowing through his tube while he lies in his cot or on our laps, we have to cuddle him as he cries while trying to hold a syringe of milk above his head. With two people this is just about manageable. In the evenings we often end up doing a kind of dance where I hold Ben tight to my chest, upright, singing him songs, while James holds the syringe of milk just above us. We have to be close because the tube isn't long and James has to mirror my swaying so the milk doesn't spill. On my own it is really difficult. His crying increases the pressure in his abdomen which forces the milk back up the tube, so gravity isn't sufficient to make it flow into his stomach. Feeds take longer and the syringe needs to be held higher above my head. I sit on the sofa with my knees bent and Ben lying against my thighs, reclined a little and facing me, so I can distract him during feeds while I watch daytime TV. We are given a bulky blue chair for him which we put on the kitchen table and it helps if he is kept upright, but he is still miserable.

At night, Ben sleeps in a cot at the foot of our bed and we set an alarm for either James or me to wake up in the night to get the milk ready and crouch next to his cot to feed him. Ben wakes as the milk fills his stomach and it is hard to get him back to sleep. I hold his hands still with one hand while keeping the milk in the air with the other. He startles easily and any noise in the house makes his arms shoot up, endangering the milk connected to the tube.

My mum encourages me to leave the house with Ben. I have taken him out locally but she suggests we get the bus to Tate Modern. It's an uneventful journey though I am tense about getting the buggy on the bus and wondering when Ben, now six weeks old, will start crying. When we arrive we ignore all art and go straight to the café. I sit by a small table on an inconveniently low armchair with Ben's buggy next to me. He is starting to grumble and frown and I presume he is hungry. My mum gets tea and pastries while I unpack the syringes, pH strips and milk that I need to feed Ben. He is on my lap as I connect syringes to the end of his tube then hold his milk vertically in the air, trying to keep it away from his arms.

Mum returns with the pastries and she cuts my croissant up for me so I can eat with one hand. A friend walks past and is thrilled to see Ben. It's the first time she has met him. 'Hello! This must be Ben. So lovely to meet him. How are you all?' she asks.

I'm pleased to see her but it's hard for my brain to tear itself away from Ben balancing on my lap and the milk in danger of being spilt. I'm on tenterhooks for the moment he starts crying. 'We're good,' I say quickly as my mum takes over the conversation. It's the first time I have fed Ben away from a hospital or home and I'm concentrating so much on getting it right, not causing a fuss, that I don't see whether anyone has noticed all of our paraphernalia. I don't want to know.

James and I are trying to work out how to look after Ben now we don't have doctors and nurses around us all the time. We are referred to our local child development centre and a team of therapists come round together to meet Ben, James and me. We sit in my parents' sitting room as they introduce themselves as physio, occupational and speech and language therapists. 'When he is awake but not agitated or hungry,' the physio says, 'you could try these exercises.' I nod and say I'll try, but there are almost no moments when Ben is not being fed or agitated or asleep. In the few moments that he is awake and quiet it is because we are rocking him, soothing him. I am too preoccupied with just getting through a day, or a night, feeding him with a bottle and a tube, to truly focus on anything else.

We have colonized my parents' house, filling their kitchen with syringes and bottles and their spare bedroom with nappies and babygros. I don't cook a single meal or do any washing. I just try to keep Ben alive.

We need to decide where to live. We have numerous conversations about whether we can return to Doha – to our flat, our friends and weekends in the desert. We aren't sure what medical help Ben needs and whether we can get it in Doha. Eventually the draw of all our family in London, now-familiar doctors and a health service that we understand wins and we decide to stay. James returns to Doha one last time to pack up our lives, bringing back one suitcase of our most urgently needed belongings and shipping the rest back more slowly.

Welcoming as they are, we can't live with my parents for ever so we find somewhere to rent nearby. When Ben is almost 12 weeks old we move into a flat at the top of a building on the peak of a hill. We can't quite afford it, and the long flights of stairs aren't hugely practical with a baby and bags of stuff, but it feels right.

Our new flat has large sash windows looking out into the still-bare branches of mature trees, high above everyone else's windows. Most of our belongings are somewhere on the ocean so we quickly unpack the few things we have brought from my parents' house and Doha, mainly things for Ben. The walls are white and the carpet grey, and the minimalism of the decoration is exactly what I need. We borrow a sofa bed from my parents to sleep on and buy a rail for our clothes (mine mostly new since my maternity clothes are now too big), a sofa to sit on and a small TV to watch. James gets a new job in London, still working for the Foreign Office. In the dim mornings of March, the flat glows yellowy orange before filling with light. On days when Ben and I barely leave the flat, between feeds and visits from therapists, I sway him from side to side while looking out of the windows at the people below and the Georgian houses opposite. I'm grateful that, for all the unexpected turns our lives have taken, we get to live in a flat like this. We fill our kitchen with Ben's feeding equipment and James's mum, Prudence, comes over to wash his syringes for us before taking Ben so I can rest.

When our shipped belongings arrive in the country we retrieve our crockery, cutlery, bed and clothes before James rents a van and takes the rest to a barn belonging to some friends. The flat can't accommodate everything we had in our large, modern apartment in Doha, and anyway, we don't need most of it. I don't want to unpack boxes of memories and work out where to put framed pictures. We are in an odd, unexpected period.

We stay in the flat for a year, as the surrounding trees come into full leaf which muffles the street noises from below. We often don't close the blinds and when we do they are translucent, so I always know how bright or grey it is outside and exactly what time of day it is. In spring, ladybirds emerge from the architraves of the windows and even this infestation feels benign. In summer we open the windows wide and I sit on the step down to a small terrace with Ben on my lap. When it snows the following winter the light changes again, as if lit from below rather than above. On New Year's Eve, James wakes me at midnight to watch the fireworks across London from our bedroom window. The flat is a calm, elegant backdrop to all the difficulties in the first year of Ben's life.

When Ben is a few months old I arrange to meet a friend, Sophie, in Hyde Park on a sunny day in spring. I arrive in the rose garden before her and it's time to feed Ben so I get started with him in the buggy. Ben starts to cry. I know that he won't calm down unless I hold him, and the milk won't go down unless he stops crying, so with one hand trying not to spill the milk in the syringe I unclip his buggy straps with the other and lift him out. Although lovely weather, it is windy which Ben doesn't like and I am trying to bob him up and down while shielding him from the breeze. My hair keeps blowing into my face but I don't have a free hand to push it back.

Sophie is a paediatric nurse. She arrives and takes in the scene, and asks, 'Why don't you have a feeding pump?'

'What's a feeding pump?' I ask, as she takes hold of the buggy and we start to walk towards a café.

'It's a little pump that you can connect to the end of Ben's tube and it will feed the milk to him. You can carry it around in a little backpack. You wouldn't have to hold the milk in the air,' she says.

It sounds like some kind of miracle.

I make some calls immediately and our dietician confirms we can have a pump. When I ask why no one had offered this to us before, she says some parents dislike using feeding pumps because they feel too medical. 'They don't want machines feeding their child, they prefer to do it themselves,' she says. I resent not being offered the choice of a pump sooner and being left to find out about it by chance because it changes our lives completely, for the better. The pump allows us to feed Ben steadily, at a carefully calibrated rate. We can go for walks while he is being fed, the pump hung in its bag from the handles of the buggy. The pressure of the pump is enough to counteract Ben's upset so he gets calories even when crying.

We can now entertain Ben while he's being fed, or distract him from his discomfort, by reading *That's Not My Car* for the hundredth time, book in one hand, my other hand available to turn the page. I prise open his fingers and help him to feel the lumpy hubcaps and shiny windows. We move through the rest of the series as the books are gifted to us by friends who see how much Ben loves them. *That's Not My Reindeer...My Monster...My Plane.* He is interested in the books and when we read them in a particular singsong voice he smiles. It feels like a breakthrough.

Despite what feels like hard work for limited results, Ben is actually reasonably healthy. The therapists we see won't talk about him having cerebral palsy because they like to wait and see before confirming, but it's obvious that Ben's reflexes and movements are not typical. He only turns his head to the right, not the left, and his body is often stiff but his head is always floppy. He has curly hair and is more beautiful than I could have imagined. It feels magical that James and I have combined to make an actual child. When he is four months old he laughs and it is one of the loveliest sounds I have ever heard.

One morning, I'm carrying Ben down the stairs from our flat when I bump into the neighbour who lives below us with her baby. She looks upset and I ask if she is OK. 'It's just that she won't stop crying,' she says, looking at her grizzly baby. 'She has never done this before and I don't know what to do.'

Her baby is a similar age to Ben, four or five months old, and I know she can hear Ben crying often from her flat. 'Oh, I'm sorry. Have you tried going for a walk?' I ask. I don't know what else to say because I have no idea what you might do with a baby who is so rarely upset. I didn't know it was even possible to be this many months into being a parent and never have seen your child inconsolable. A few months later, she invites us round for tea and, while Ben sits on my lap with his feeding pump nearby, she peels a satsuma for her daughter and offers her individual segments which her daughter holds neatly and then brings deftly to her mouth. I am hypnotized by the simplicity and complexity of it.

I think about the son I had imagined during pregnancy, who wouldn't have had to struggle to do the most basic things. I feel cheated that I should have spent time with my newborn but wasn't able to hold him for five days. It has been by far the most traumatic thing that has ever happened to me and I am reeling while also realizing I had led a fortunate life. Some days are OK and some days are a struggle.

A relative wrote to us when they found out about Ben and said it was times like these that made you realize what it was to love and be loved. I love Ben so much I sometimes feel my heart might burst, but I feel overwhelmed. I rely completely on our families, a few friends and James. He and I met at university and have been together for ten years. His support and love are unwavering, holding me up.

I get little flashes where I am shocked by how much things have changed in such a short period of time. I didn't think

I would be raising my baby in London. When I take Ben to the baby clinic there is a woman whispering in Arabic to her baby – 'Mashallah, mashallah' – and it's so familiar but feels out of context. A car drives past our window with the call to prayer playing so loudly that I think, just for a moment, that I am in Damascus or Doha again. I know London is the right place for us but I miss the life we were meant to have when our baby would be familiar with the muezzin's call and weaned on falafel.

When Ben is six months old, I take him to Spain with my family while James stays in London to work. I take a trunk full of feeding supplies, milk and various medications. I'm nervous about security at the airport but the only thing that causes issues is the pair of nail scissors that my mum has in her hand luggage.

We are staying with family friends in a remote, self-built house in a forest. It's a few hours from the airport and Ben screams so much in the hire car on the way there that he makes himself sick. In the UK we try to do most journeys by train to avoid this happening but here there is no other option. We stop a number of times, but each time we get back in the car he screams again, turning himself bright red, and eventually I decide we'll just have to keep on driving and only stop if he chokes. I am very stressed but there's no alternative. I feel like I make decisions like this all the time now which aren't about making Ben happy but about doing what's necessary.

I have been coming to this place on holiday since my childhood and I know it well. We park on the track above the house and carry our luggage down to the gate to the smallholding. There are three houses spread out among the trees, with a pond, chickens and pigs. The houses are white and filled with trinkets collected on our friends' travels and pots they have made. The buildings are basic but comfortable and each time I return I remember how beautiful they are as I walk around noticing new bits that have been built since my last visit. Ben sleeps in a travel cot on the floor of the main room of our house, while my bed is up steep, uneven stone steps on a mezzanine. Ben has milk at 11pm so, as everyone heads off to bed, I connect the pump and hold Ben's hands through the side of the cot. During the night I return when he wakes. In the morning my mum gets up with Ben and I hear her talking softly to him before she takes him past the avocado tree to the house next door for his breakfast. I drift back to sleep despite the sun creeping through the thin curtains. My mum and middle sister Maddy help a lot, but I feel James's absence. I'm glad when he arrives a week later to share parenting responsibility unquestioningly. I feel lighter with him there.

I bring with us a particular squeaky toy which Ben likes having waved in front of him as he sits on our laps. We read *Goodnight Moon*, showing him the bright pictures that I hope he can see. In Ben's early months, an eye doctor had told us that he might not be able to see well. 'I'll give you this leaflet about cortical blindness,' he had said, and I had been shocked because I felt like Ben could see. I thought his sight had been spared and if it hadn't then I should, at some gut level, have realized. I know that contrasting colours are good for babies and *Goodnight Moon* has bright, graphic pictures. I am convinced Ben is looking at them meaningfully and I hope I am right. We move the squeaky toy, with its black-and-white fabric and bright red nose, from side to side, encouraging Ben's head to track the movement, and he can do it. It's jolty and inconsistent but I'm sure he's looking.

Since Ben can't roll or sit, I lay him in the middle of the large dining table by open windows with draping bougainvillea, looking at dressers full of handmade colourful pottery. This is the table that we sat around when I was a teenager, while my parents chatted to their friends and mosquitoes nipped at our ankles. I find a bucket to bathe Ben in and luckily the solar panels have heated enough water to fill it. I put the bucket on the terrace overlooking the cork trees below and hold him with my hands so he doesn't slip down as our friends' dogs come over to sniff his head.

When I was a teenager we often walked down through the surrounding cork forest to the local village. To begin with I did it begrudgingly, forced by my parents, but over the years I came to appreciate the calmness of the forest and liked seeing the trees that looked naked at the base of their trunks where the cork bark had been stripped off. I want to do the walk again, with my new family. It would be impossible with a buggy but we think we can manage it with Ben in a sling, so James, Ben, Maddy, her boyfriend and I set off through the dappled shade, hearing the herd of goats with bells round their necks in the distance.

After half an hour or so Ben is due to be fed so we stop on a rock in the middle of the forest and pH test, connect the pump and start the milk. James carries on walking with Ben on his front in a sling and the rucksack of milk on his back. An hour later we reach the railway line at the bottom of the valley and walk into the village by the tracks, rewarding ourselves with cold beers at a bar. It is a victory to have remembered everything we need and to have learned to feed Ben in this kind of situation. It feels like the kind of thing we did on holiday before becoming parents. I'm happy to have shown James the backdrop of my childhood anecdotes and to have been able to include Ben. It is a magical trip, but not a recuperative holiday. I am constantly aware of what I need to do, or what Ben will need shortly. I am constantly anxious about anything going wrong.

Once we return from Spain, Ben turns six months old and it is clear to everyone that he isn't going to be able to drink or eat enough to keep himself alive. There is the possibility of a gastrostomy, where a hole is made in the abdomen so a long-term feeding device can be fitted between the skin and the stomach itself. Rather than milk flowing via his nose, it could go straight into his stomach via a different tube. Doctors, nurses and therapists have talked to us about this gently, wary of our reaction to surgery and permanent incisions, but we are keen. The NG tube is a source of near-constant anxiety to us and discomfort to Ben. Our attempts to help him learn to drink milk, and recently to eat food, have not been successful enough to keep him nourished. Surgery to fit a gastrostomy will be painful in the short term but surely better in the long term and will allow me to stop pushing tubes up his nose. We ask for it to happen as soon as possible.

Asking to have a tube inserted into your baby's tummy is a strange request. It will mean we'll have to send Ben into the operating theatre alone and there are risks with surgery. We will have to nurse him through recovery and afterwards there will always be a tube dangling from his abdomen. But there isn't an option where Ben doesn't have to have any kind of feeding tube. We only have a choice between a tube on his face or a tube in his tummy and after six months of the tube in his nose we are ready for an alternative. I want to be able to kiss and cuddle him without worrying about dislodging the tube and I don't want to worry about whether I'll have to push a new tube down all the time. Just worrying about the actual feeding, rather than the tube itself, will feel like progress for us.

We are given a date for surgery. We have to take Ben into hospital the day before the operation so doctors can check he is well and take blood in preparation for surgery. We sign the necessary forms and then there is nothing to do except wait for the morning. Being back in hospital with Ben is difficult. We are in a paediatric ward this time and in some ways it's different to the neonatal unit – not least because we are expected to be with Ben all the time. There are not enough nurses to keep an eye on him when he isn't being given medication or observed. The sense of having no control over light, heat, air and noise is the same. We live close to the hospital and so they allow us to go and sleep that night in our own beds, on the understanding that we will return early the next morning.

When we arrive at 7am we wait. Ben is put in a gown and when they are ready for us a few hours later, I carry him along the corridor and down in the lift while James and a nurse push his cotbed. I hold Ben as they put a tiny mask over his face and he drifts off then lay him onto the waiting bed. When he had tests or procedures as a newborn we were part-time parents, leaving him alone in hospital for some portion of each day, but now Ben is with me all the time, and leaving him in the operating room, looking vulnerable under the bright lights, is painful. We are told it will be at least an hour before Ben is out of theatre and that we should wait on the ward. There, they say we can leave our mobile numbers and they will call us when the operation is finished.

We know from our overfamiliarity with the hospital that there are some areas that don't get any mobile reception so we go and sit on a wall outside, drinking tea and trying not to dwell on thoughts of Ben lying on a big bed being cut open. After almost an hour, I worry that even though our phones are clearly working the ward may be trying to call us and we go back inside. As we walk into the ward, we can hear a nurse on the phone saying, 'No, we haven't told Ben's parents to come down because no one told us to.' By the time we get to the recovery area, Ben is distraught with unfamiliar deep-throated sobs that stop briefly and then restart. We cannot pick him up so we stand on either side of the bed and hold his hands and stroke his cheeks.

With the nurses on the ward we are largely able to manage his discomfort that afternoon and evening. I sleep on a camp bed next to his cot, waking every time a nurse checks him, until James and Maddy arrive in the morning so I can go home for a nap. Staying in hospital is a strange mix of stressful and boring. When Ben is obviously in pain and needs help, we're glad to be there and worried about him. When he improves, keeping down milk and smiling, it feels restrictive. We have got used to being parents on our own but now we are back to co-parenting with medics and it feels infantilizing.

When Ben is miserable he tells us so by sticking out his bottom lip, which is endearing and heartbreaking. Our usual technique of soothing him by cradling him across our body and swaying is difficult because his tummy is so sore. This is the first time we have had to nurse Ben in an overtly medical way. He has always been intact; there have never been wounds. I find it difficult dealing with the raw hole in his tummy now and don't know what to expect. I am told the site of the tube will heal happily, like an ear piercing, but it feels unlikely. I miss being able to hold him upright and cuddle him properly.

The feeding nurse, Ellen, comes to show us how to feed Ben. We first met her when Ben was a week old and I was expressing milk. She showed me the pumping room in the neonatal unit and how to sterilize the pump. Now she shows us how to feed Ben with this new tube and it is so wonderfully simple. Because the tube is anchored in his stomach there is no need to check the pH and no danger of it falling out. We can just unclamp the tube, flush through a little water and then give him milk. The day after the operation everything is going well and we are discharged by the evening. I am relieved to escape the confines of the hospital.

At home we are all exhausted. James goes back to work the next day but Ben is even less settled than normal and I can hear a bubbling noise around the new hole in his tummy which is disconcerting. I don't know if that is normal and I decide to take him to A&E since that is the only way of us seeing a doctor quickly. A surgeon comes and tightens the tube against Ben's stomach and we return home, nervous but reassured.

The following day Ben is still really unhappy. As I feed him on my lap on the sofa I feel wet. We are both sitting in a puddle of milk which is leaking from his stomach and I assume this must be wrong. I am so upset that Ben is in pain, and that there is milk leaking where it shouldn't be. I don't want to return to hospital when I thought we had reclaimed our freedom but I need someone to check the tube.

When we get there, we are seen by a surgeon who is not worried, almost dismissive. He tells me he will give Ben antibiotics in case the milk leaked somewhere inside his body that isn't his stomach, and he will tighten the tube again. We will need to stay in hospital for another night or two. James is there as much as he can be but he's under huge pressure at work, so Maddy and her friend Helen devote their days to keeping me company. Maddy is my younger sister by five years but has always seemed older than that. She is optimistic and funny and she and Helen joke about the doctors and tell me stories about their friends to keep me from going mad.

When Ben is tired Maddy climbs into his cot and they fall asleep squished together. Helen sits on the floor, as there is only one chair, with a stack of magazines, offering cups of tea at regular intervals. I am desperate to go home, but also wary of Ben's misery and freaked out by the apparent permeability of his stomach. I am used to Ben's milk reappearing through his mouth, but for it to leak out of this hole is unsettling.

When we make it home things have stabilized. Over the following months there are ups and downs with the new tube. It gets sore and the nurses I see are unhelpful. I take against a junior surgeon in A&E who pokes Ben's sore stomach unnecessarily while telling us in complicated words that it is inflamed. I wonder if this permanent tube is really better than the one he had on his face but I gradually work out who to call if there is a problem: Ellen, the specialist nurse.

Ellen taught us to feed Ben at each stage and continues to shepherd us through issues as they arise. I gradually become more confident in looking after the new tube and it is a lifeline. It is the reason that Ben thrives and grows. It represents a choice to spend time reading books and getting outside rather than balancing syringes of milk or trying for hours to get enough calories into Ben via his mouth. We can spend more time on the things he enjoys. At seven months he has preferences for songs, like 'Row, Row, Row Your Boat', but not 'Twinkle Twinkle Little Star', and smiles at those he enjoys. He likes to be held a particular way. He knows James and me and smiles in recognition. When we are in a café he makes shouting noises until a lady acknowledges him. Two tiny teeth appear in his lower gums and I am reminded that in some ways he is an entirely typical baby.

I am not working and, combined with living in London unexpectedly and Ben's complications, we are spending more money than we have. I find out I can apply for Disabled Living Allowance for Ben, a state benefit which will help us with the additional costs of his condition. I get the form and fill out all 40 pages, using extra space at the back to list all of the professionals involved in Ben's care. I attach letters from doctors, prescription lists and test results. I have been told the decision will rest on how much additional care Ben needs compared with a typical baby of a similar age and I'm not sure whether he will qualify. A family worker at a local charity tells me I should keep a diary of a typical day and night and use this to answer the questions in minute detail, so I note that it takes us five minutes, three times a day to dress him after a nap, but only three minutes, three times a day to undress him. I tell them, 'We spend 30 minutes, 3 times a day preparing Ben's milk and food. We spend 95 minutes, 5 times a day tube feeding him.' I am pleased when the form asks, 'Does he have difficulty hearing?' so that there is at least one box that I can just tick 'no' to and not need to fill out paragraphs of additional explanation. Six weeks later I receive a letter confirming Ben is eligible for the highest rate of DLA.

A few months after his operation, when he is nine months old, I give Ben his usual bath then lay him on top of a towel on our dining table while I cover him in lotions. His fat cheeks are clear, though shiny from cream, and the sandpapery roughness of eczema has given way to smooth porcelain skin. The area around his tube is no longer red though I still put a little antibacterial cream around it. Ben holds his arms, hands fisted, up at 90 degrees, as if he's about to lift a barbell above his head. He has chubby creases at his wrists, mid-forearms and mid-thighs. He cannot lift his head, or roll, or hold onto anything, but I don't know what a typical nine-month-old would be doing. As I'm massaging cream into his legs, I list names from his favourite programme, *In the Night Garden*, in a funny voice. He will watch TV for short periods now and I am so grateful for it. Every time I reach the end, saying the name of his favourite character, 'Makka Pakka!', he giggles. As I start the joke again he chuckles a little bit in encouragement and then waits for the end to dissolve into peals of laughter, his eyes almost disappearing beneath the fulsome cheeks pushed up by his grin. He is the epitome of a happy baby.

I had always wondered whether if something cataclysmic happened I would suddenly realize I did believe in God, or find some previously unexplored belief system to support me. I had been vaguely intrigued by how it would feel to find myself in a truly difficult situation and now I know. I still don't believe in anything divine, but I appear to be putting one foot in front of the other despite many aspects of my life feeling unrecognizable. I seem to be resilient, and I'm pleased. Rather than finding the demands of parenting impossible, it is the relentless demands that keep me going. I am being held together by my love for my son and my family's love for me, and my husband who I cling to like a limpet. I had always been proudly independent, despite having been with my husband for so long, but now I feel fragile. I couldn't possibly do it alone. My outer layer has been sloughed away by Ben's birth and now I'm exposed to all of the difficulty, unfairness and sadness of life.

3

In spring, I had gone with a friend to a baby massage class, one of eight mothers who laid their babies on the floor in front of them. We were given massage oils and shown how to move our hands across our babies' tummies to help with colic. As I tried to copy what we were shown, Ben started to cry. I shushed him gently but I was unable to do much more massaging. When Ben lay on his back on a flat surface, no matter how soft, he looked unmoored. His legs and arms moved all the time like he was trying to work out where the perimeter of his body was in the absence of anything to push against. Gravity didn't seem to be sufficient to weigh down his limbs. He didn't want to be massaged, he wanted to be held firmly, to be shown where his edges were. I avoided going to other local baby groups. Our days were so full of feeding and appointments there was barely any time to go anywhere and when I did try it didn't go well.

By the time the tube on his face was gone the gap between what Ben could do with his body and what other babies his age could do had widened, which often meant sympathetic or inquisitive questions and I didn't want to answer them. If I said Ben had cerebral palsy people sometimes mistook it for cystic fibrosis and I ended up explaining the difference between the two conditions even though I didn't really know what cystic fibrosis was. Sometimes people would tilt their head slightly to the side when I explained Ben's condition and look at me with pity. Often they would apologize, though it wasn't clear what for. Physically helping Ben in these situations, while juggling my own emotions and managing other people's responses, was too much. I consoled myself that Ben didn't get enough out of the groups to miss them.

I found one story group at a local library which did work for us. It was small and at a time that worked between feeds. Parents and their babies sat on the scruffy carpet and a librarian read stories. They had special books which were enormous, bigger than the babies. Ben listened carefully to *Dear Zoo*. Halfway through the story session, a basket of percussion appeared. Most of the other babies crawled around helping themselves to rattles while I reached over Ben to grab a shaker. He sat on my lap and I stretched open his fist to put the shaker in his fingers and then closed my hand over his so it wouldn't escape. He smiled as we sang songs and he extended his body back as he got excited by the ones he particularly liked. He was small enough that when he straightened his body in excitement I could easily push back with my chest against his back and close him back up, hinging his hips to put him in a seated position once more. I lifted his arms above his head to whoosh them down as we sang about the spider getting washed out of the water spout and he gave out a little shriek of glee. He loved the feeling of his limbs being moved firmly, fast, like it was only these big movements that his body could appreciate. As the session came to an end we all stood in a circle and sang the 'Hokey Cokey'. We worked through each limb, putting our 'right arm in', then our left, before each leg. We span around, and every time we got to the chorus I swept Ben up and away from me in my outstretched arms: 'Oohh, the Hokey Cokey!' He laughed more than any of the other babies.

We spend hours getting Ben to sleep for naps and at night, rocking him or holding his hands as he lies on his side in his cot. If he falls asleep in his buggy he wakes as soon as a police car goes past, his arms shooting up as he startles at the noise, or if someone makes a coffee in a café. We are on tenterhooks whenever he's asleep, wondering how long it will be until he wakes up.

One day, we visit some friends who put their younger child down for a nap while we're there. He's a similar age to Ben and they take him upstairs, put him in his cot and he goes to sleep. I am so distracted by the ease of this that I can't concentrate properly on our conversation. I had no idea it could be that straightforward. I never relax, even when Ben is sleeping, like both of us are continually primed for threat, though it seems Ben is sabotaging himself. His body appears to make him unhappy, it wakes itself or shocks itself and I don't know what to do about it.

One afternoon I am crossing the road and a teenage boy runs in front of us, bashing into Ben's buggy and I scream at him. He tells me to 'f★★k off' and I am outraged, but also shocked at myself. As the adrenaline dissipates I know that Ben was never in danger, I had overreacted, but it was like I was on high alert for trouble.

As Ben approaches ten months old, I spend most of each day feeding him. We're doing regular milk feeds via the pump into his tummy and also feeding him thickened purées on a spoon three times a day, which is slow and messy. We are awake regularly throughout the night with him and there is little let-up in the intensity of his needs, but Ben is spending moments of each day happy. We have ways to entertain and distract him with TV, books and jokes. We can make him smile and laugh easily by pretending to sneeze or talking in silly voices. We have found toys that he can bash if they are put in front of him, though his arms don't really do what he wants them to. We have moments of calm, when Ben sometimes makes little clicking noises as his tongue moves backward and forward in his mouth.

I take Ben for a walk each day, whether on the way to an appointment or just to leave the house. As I push his buggy I listen, constantly though not always consciously, for the telltale noise which means he has mismanaged the co-ordination of swallowing and breathing and is choking. When I hear it, I hurriedly put on the buggy's brakes so he doesn't roll away and I quickly move to the front of the buggy and undo the straps in order to tip Ben forward before his lips get any bluer. After a moment, the strangled noise stops and he takes a big gasp of air. The choking often happens when it is windy and the shock of a gust muddles his breathing. Sometimes it happens for no apparent reason, which is actually caused by his reflux. Reflux is the bane of his and our lives. Ben chokes in pubs, lifts and when he's in bed. Sometimes he vomits when he recovers his breath, sometimes he doesn't. We get used to it and it's one more thing that we learn to manage.

I can't work out how to talk about Ben's disability in social situations. I try to get a balance between the medical stuff and the baby things. In spite of the complexity of feeding, moving, sleeping, he is just a baby. He has new teeth. He loves 'The Wheels on the Bus'. He has chubby cheeks and curly hair, like Harry Styles, Dr M says. I think he's the most delicious baby I have ever seen. When strangers talk to Ben in his buggy he looks fairly typical and I can choose how much to tell them, at least until they try to give him something and I have to explain that he can't hold the toy they are offering.

We help him to play with toys, putting a rattle into his hand which he shakes until it drops out. He can just about knock over a tower of bricks that we have built. 'Boof!' we say, to try and encourage him to hit things, 'Just boof it, Ben!' I see him brace for the noise of the blocks collapsing, which will make him jump. We accumulate plastic cups and wooden animals. We know he also likes songs, particularly when adults do the actions, but books are his favourite. We are building up our collection. *Shark in the Park* has a line about Timothy Pope and his telescope and we realize Ben loves the patterns of words, the repetition of phrases. We read about the shark at home while Ben is propped on his tummy, encouraging him to lift up his head to see. A friend gives us a musical book of *Wheels on the Bus* and we take this everywhere we go, unbothered by how much noise we make, just relieved that Ben is engaged and quiet. At the end of this book a series of teddies say goodbye to the bus and Ben gives a little chuckle each time we read it. I love the predictability of it – that every day, if I like, I can get him to make that little chuckle by reading that book. Even on bad days that book can at least raise a smile.

I feel like it should be easier to speak to people we know well but when talking to a friend whose child had an operation I compare our experiences and he seems shocked. He points out how different his child is to Ben, that his child doesn't have any other problems except needing a minor operation. He could just mean, sympathetically, that his child is less complicated than mine, but I think he is shocked that I have compared his non-disabled daughter with my disabled son. I don't seem to have a way into these conversations – there is so much that is unfamiliar to the people we know that I don't know where to start. It's easier to be positive and talk about how well Ben's doing, which is true but not the whole story. James copies me into an email to a friend where he briefly updates him on Ben and describes our days as 'extremely tiring for all concerned' and he is right.

After nine months of motherhood I start thinking about returning to work and am offered a job by the architectural practice I worked for before we left for the Middle East. I am torn between my self-imposed expectation that I would return to work after I had a baby and feeling that Ben needs me. The intensity of that need is also why I want to return to work. I want to do everything for him and yet I feel suffocated by being his mother all the time. My employers are flexible and I think working part time will allow me to feel like a competent grown-up in a world beyond my son. I am jealous of James leaving for work in the morning and not being responsible for another human until the afternoon. I crave an opportunity to not be someone's mother, just for a bit.

I look into childcare for Ben and meet a potential childminder. She shows me her childcare certificates as Ben sits on my lap. I look at her pristine carpet beneath my puke-prone child as Ben cranes to watch her TV and I listen to her say she can manage all of Ben's needs while she looks after another toddler and collects other children from school. It could be that she can multitask in a way that I have not discovered, but I find it hard to do everything I am meant to with Ben each day, on my own, and I decide she cannot look after him. I visit a nursery, hoping that having a team of staff might be better for him and them, but it's clear they are intimidated by Ben's tube feeding and how much care he requires. They tell me they have a very long waiting list and would need to secure additional funding for Ben. I leave with the impression they do not want him there.

I had put Ben's name down for a second local nursery but have heard nothing. I phone to check and happen to speak to the manager. 'Tell me about your son,' she says. While I explain our situation she listens and suggests I visit. 'One of our girls is about to leave for school. She also has special needs, so perhaps Ben could take her place. Would Thursdays and Fridays work for you?' I am willing to accept whatever days we can get. We have no other options — we can't afford a nanny and I can't find a childminder.

The nursery is well worn with doorframes that have been painted and repainted then bashed again so the new chips are multicoloured. The corridor down towards the baby room is narrow and we take off our shoes before we go in. The woman who will be Ben's keyworker, Anita, has a wide, welcoming, gap-toothed grin and frequently rumbles with laughter. When she talks Ben's arms leap up as he startles at the volume of her voice. I listen carefully to what Anita says, hoping she shares her manager's enthusiasm for including Ben, and I think she does. She listens attentively as I show her how to feed Ben and tell her what he likes. All of the practitioners in the room have worked there for years. They have a no-nonsense dedication to their work which is both intimidating and comforting: Annie is abrupt and doesn't smile and I worry she thinks Ben is too complicated and I am too fussy. Imogen is quiet and younger, softer than the others. She pays close attention while quietly wiping noses and proffering toys.

On his first day, I stay with Ben at nursery, sitting quietly in a corner, as we watch the other babies crawl and stand. On the second day I leave him for an hour. As I walk the short distance to our flat, I call James in tears: 'There's no way we can leave Ben there. They don't know how to look after him. I can't go back to work.'

'Why don't we give it a couple of days and see how it goes?' James suggests.

We do and it just about works. There are various discussions and doubts, from them and us in the first few weeks. I spend a great deal of time there showing the staff how I look after him. I try to explain that sometimes Ben has good days, sometimes bad. Ben's physiotherapist arranges for a specialist chair to be delivered to the nursery and when he sits in it he can see everyone but I worry that he might be left in it too much. Just like filling in the forms for the Disabled Living Allowance, teaching the nursery how to look after him brings home how much there is to do each day: tube feeding, bottle or cup feeding, giving him purée on a spoon, physio exercises and sensory tasks to practise. We are meant to be working with Ben on every area of his development: drinking, eating, sitting up, rolling, head control, communicating, sleeping. It's a full schedule when he is well and happy, almost impossible when he's not. I tell the nursery that when he is sad the only thing that will comfort him is to be held and swayed, but I don't know if this is a reasonable request. I can see Anita absorbing all that I tell her and I begin to believe this might work.

I go to work two days a week, when Ben isn't ill and doesn't have appointments (or ones that James can take him to). On the nights before I work, I sleep on a mattress on the sitting room floor with ear plugs in, leaving James to get up with

Ben in the night and get him to nursery in the morning. I catch the train early, leaving in the dark. I'm amazed by the ease of walking down stairs to the station without a buggy. I read books on the tube, slipping through just-closing doors. At work I go to the loo alone and my colleagues are undemanding. At lunchtime I walk to buy a sandwich, excited by the range of options at a small supermarket, and eat at my desk with two hands and what feels like all the time in the world but is actually 15 minutes. I have conversations that aren't about Ben, where people don't call me 'mum'. I feel like I am coming back to myself – spending days continuing an architectural career I had spent eight years qualifying for.

Even though I'm with Ben less, I still find some of my days at home with him hard. He is upset frequently, sometimes for hours. It is hard to distract him since feeding is no comfort and he can't suck a dummy. It's hard to tell if he is made miserable by teething, reflux, viruses or all three. We aren't getting much sleep. We go to lots of appointments, trying to narrow down the things we can improve for him. While I am arranging time off work for one doctor appointment I send an email to James: 'Shall we both go to this one since things are so awful?' When we discuss his distress with doctors they often say it is probably reflux and will likely improve as he gets older. But just waiting until he's older for everything to magically resolve itself feels hopeless. We are trying to work out how we can make Ben's life better and then teach the nursery what we know, but some of it is impossible. 'He's been quite upset today,' his keyworker says as I collect him one afternoon, 'I'm not sure why.'

'Me neither,' I say as I gather up our bags. I want to have the solution to Ben's sadness but I don't.

Sometimes Ben is upset when I collect him, but increasingly not as the months wear on. He often vomits and they learn how to deal with it. Some days he sleeps, though not reliably. Colds and coughs come and go, directly affecting Ben's mood, and are documented in the notebook that we send back and forth. 'Too much flames,' Anita writes one day and while I know she means phlegm, I am sympathetic to her description.

Occasionally when I collect Ben he will be curled up in the corner of a room on a mat, covered with blankets and oblivious to the noise around him. He would never sleep somewhere this noisy at home and I'm amazed, relieved that he's getting some rest. Sometimes everyone will be in the big garden and I look out for Ben among the older children running around and find him on the swing, bolstered with rolled up blankets, in the shadow of what was once the grandest house in the area. Or sitting with staff under a tree. Anita fusses around him, mimicking the clicking noise he makes. 'Ah, here's your Dolphin Boy,' she says as I approach. Other kids tear around the garden on bikes, leaping from climbing frames; I am sad Ben can't ride the bikes but happy that he's here with all these energetic kids.

When I pick Ben up, he smells of all the women who care for him there and not at all like my son. I know this means that he has been held for most of the day, close enough to absorb some of their perfume, and I am relieved that my worries about him being left uncuddled are unfounded, but it's still odd that he doesn't smell like my son. I take him home to bathe and reclaim him.

The nursery isn't perfect. It is sometimes disorganized and is constantly threatened with restructuring by the council. I have to pull the staff up on things occasionally – like when I find Ben facing away from all the other children when I arrive one afternoon – but they react well to my concerns and through it all we never doubt that Ben is welcome. The women who look after Ben are dedicated to him, showering him with attention and affection. They are committed and I love the way they try. They juggle resources to make sure Ben has someone with him, even when the funding they are being given is insufficient, because Ben needs more attention than other kids.

At nursery and at home we keep trying different toys, thinking that he might be able to enjoy this one or that, but it's almost impossible for Ben to play with any of them on his own and he is mainly uninterested or annoyed. It is ironic that he needs to be able to play and entertain himself more than other babies because he can't crawl or investigate things himself, yet finds it so hard to play. He doesn't have the distraction of rolling across the floor or pulling himself up to stand, like other children use Ben's buggy to do. He needs us to provide all of those opportunities to explore, to help him use his fingers and open his pudgy hands. Combined with the worry and exhaustion of keeping him fed and not miserable and conversations about feeding tubes and reflux, gross motor skills and postural support, it is a lot. But we are finding moments of joy.

We are getting to know Ben's inner life – his sense of humour and his interests. Books are joyful. Jokes are a relief. Some stories or funny phrases can make him laugh to the point of hysteria, though sometimes he tips from hilarity to sobbing, as though he has crested a wave of high emotion and has now been plunged into sadness, which seems unfair. If we keep him on the fun side of laughter he often gets hiccups. 'He's exactly like you,' James says. 'I've never known anyone get hiccups from laughing as reliably as you.' When Ben was in my womb I had wondered what the rhythmical pulses in my swollen belly were until a midwife told me it was the foetus hiccupping. I was amazed that *in utero* babies hiccupped. Now I feel like these hiccups are one thing that is unchanged from how I thought of Ben in the womb and how he is now, and show incontrovertibly that he is mine.

As we learn how to make Ben laugh, or how to stop him crying, we are able to laugh ourselves. After almost a year of just keeping going, permanently tightly wound, wondering what might go wrong, when he might next wake, whether we have cleaned the syringes or whether he is about to vomit, there is more light. A little relaxing of our fraught bodies and minds, and it makes all of us feel a little less bewildered.

In November we go on holiday to Yorkshire with Maddy and her boyfriend. We take all that we need, including Ben's supportive chair and a playmat that we can make into a seat on the floor, and are relieved that we don't forget anything crucial. We stay in a farmhouse that James's family has stayed in often, in an area he is familiar with from his own childhood holidays. Ben watches programmes on a screen that is far bigger than our TV at home and he is transfixed.

We put Ben's big blue chair on the dining table in front of the fire, sometimes forgetting to do up the strap because he doesn't have the strength to pull his body forwards, and he watches us as we cook dinner in this unfamiliar room. Ben sleeps as badly as he does at home and I am often awake with him early in the morning, sitting by the Aga while the room gradually fills with strange flat light as the sun rises and we can see that the house is surrounded by snow. We hear an occasional thump as wads of snow fall from laden bare branches. When we go for a walk we carry Ben because his buggy is useless in snow and we have to look carefully to find the path in the pillowy landscape. We put him in layers of clothes, wrap him in a woollen blanket and walk to a hill that James, Maddy and her boyfriend can sled down. The last time the snow was this thick, Ben was newborn in hospital. Now he is almost a year old, thriving enough to be heavy in my arms.

When it is time to drive home, Maddy and her boyfriend shovel snow off the track out to the main road. We head slowly south on treacherous motorways with reduced visibility and we realize we can't get back to London in a day. We have to stop frequently to feed Ben and to release him from the constriction of his car seat before heading back to the slushy motorway. We decide to stay the night in Nottingham with

Maddy before driving on to London the next day. We arrive, unpack, and get Ben into the portable cot we have brought with us. I go to sleep nearby but not long afterwards James wakes me. He is worried about Ben's breathing, which is laboured. James thinks we should call an ambulance but I don't want to make a fuss. I can't tell how bad the breathing is – Ben has had similar episodes before which have sorted themselves out – but this feels unfamiliar. We decide to drive ourselves to hospital, following Maddy and her boyfriend who know the way. I don't have time to put in my contact lenses so I leave wearing my glasses, pulling on some clothes and shoving my feet into wellies on the way out.

We walk into A&E through the snow, James checking I don't slip on the ice. I am carrying Ben and I tell the receptionist that he is having problems breathing. They rush us through into a cubicle where nurses immediately start giving him oxygen. I briefly explain his medical history and various complications. Within moments, the room is full of doctors and nurses administering medicine. Ben is struggling to breathe and distressed. A doctor comes to talk to us about his condition in more detail. 'We think he has croup. We might need to sedate him,' he says. 'We will take him to intensive care if his breathing doesn't improve soon.' We are terrified. He hasn't been urgently, critically unwell since he was born and for all our rapid education in medical care, we are not prepared for this.

After the initial flurry of activity, a nurse suggests we spend some quiet time with Ben, trying to be as calm as possible. 'Let's see if the medication is working,' she says. While James attempts to keep a nebulizer close to his face, I take off my wellies and climb onto the bed, sit Ben in my lap, and start reading. We had remembered to bring *The Very Hungry Caterpillar* with us. He loves this book from my childhood, particularly the page of all the different foods that the caterpillar ate. We can usually make him laugh by reading out this list in a particular voice, a hurried tone, almost exasperated. Now, Ben doesn't laugh, but I read it slowly and deliberately, glad to have something to do, and within a couple of minutes his breathing has stabilized. He is calmer, and no longer struggling. There is a hint of a smile when we get to the list of foods – aided by drugs, but helped along by his love of the book. The nurse who has been loitering just beyond the curtain where Ben can't see her comes in. 'I have never seen such a reaction from a baby to a book!' she says.

I'm grateful for all of the medics and medicine that have helped him recover his breath and am relieved that we have helped to comfort him. Like his stay in hospital when he was a baby, we are part of the team looking after him, but now I'm one of the most important members.

I stay in hospital with him overnight so they can confirm that it was croup and that the danger has now passed. We are moved up to a ward where I am given a camp bed next to his cot. When I take my glasses off to try to sleep I can't see anything in focus and I feel uncomfortable in this unfamiliar hospital. I barely sleep and my phone runs out of battery.

In the morning, James phones the ward and the nurses tell me he is coming to collect us. The roads are still treacherous and when the doctor realizes we are planning to return to London she suggests Ben and I get the train. 'At least if the train gets stuck in the snow, you'll have other passengers to help,' she says. 'You don't want to be stuck in a car and have to carry him to safety in this freezing weather.' So James takes us to the station and I board the train. By the time we return to London we feel like we have been on an expedition and need a lifetime to recover.

In December, Ben turns one and we celebrate with our families and friends, more for us than for him. His physiotherapist arranges for a new chair for him which is neon green and height adjustable. It keeps him upright and has a tray, so we can put toys near his hands. For his birthday we buy a baby laptop which lights up and makes noises when he whacks the buttons. We put special non-stick mats underneath so it doesn't slide across the tray out of his reach. He is entranced. We have found something for him to play with!

He has new favourite TV programmes like *Boogie Beebies* where the presenters dance and *Something Special*, where Mr Tumble signs when he speaks. With the chair, the toy and the TV we can leave him for short periods of time which means I can make myself a sandwich, which is both a small thing and huge progress. We have survived his first year.

4

We are trying to unravel the mysteries of Ben's body. Ben is awake every night, often for hours, and we are exhausted. I know that it's normal for babies to not sleep reliably but it's been a year of broken nights and it feels relentless. 'I think looking after Ben is harder than looking after twins the same age, you know,' a friend says. I protest but later wonder if it is true.

I am fascinated by other people's children. Are they easier or harder to look after than Ben? I don't want to win the competition for most tricky child but I want to know if my levels of responsibility and exhaustion are typical or unusual. I think all babies wake at night. All babies need feeding and constant supervision. But exactly how much? Yet when someone says my life is difficult I deny it hotly because I can't stand the notion that Ben is difficult or that people should feel sorry for me, even though I think they are probably right.

Ben can't move himself into a comfortable position or be lulled back to sleep with milk. We try changes in position and timing. We start giving him medication and on one of the first nights that we try it he falls asleep in James's arms with no swaying or stroking. It feels almost too easy and we lay him gently in bed and gratefully spend the evening with some friends in the next room, but always with one ear out, wondering if it will last. It doesn't. We continue the medication and it mostly helps him fall asleep but it doesn't keep him asleep all night. The only thing stopping me and James losing it altogether is the one night a week Ben spends at my parents' house, when we go to sleep early, relieved that my mum is going to be awake with Ben rather than us. There is so much going on, it would be a lot even if we were well rested: adjusting to Ben being at nursery, trying to buy a house, both of us working, the appointments for Ben. So many appointments.

Just after Ben's first birthday, we leave him with James's parents and go to a wedding where most of our friends don't yet have children. Between us living abroad and having Ben, we haven't spent much time with these friends for years and it is wonderful to see people we like so much. When I talk to them I feel like the same person they have known since university. We share jokes and stories but when they ask about Ben I don't know how to explain about tube feeding and physio and the sheer intensity of it all.

I want to talk about how delightful Ben is but also how difficult some days are, how all my time is spent looking after my child or managing other aspects of his life. It's hard to articulate because I feel so different from my friends. They are still doing the kinds of things I was doing before Ben was born and that feels like a lifetime ago. I am torn between staying up late dancing at the wedding, like I would have done before I had Ben, and going to bed because I know I can sleep all night undisturbed.

Surrounded by the music and dancing, I talk to a friend of a friend who has a disabled child and all of the pieces fit into place. Suddenly I have the words and we have so much in common it feels easy and effortless. Her daughter is older than Ben and I am amazed at how together she seems, how comfortable and joyful she is when talking about her daughter. She tells me how well I am doing and I don't know if she's right but I feel buoyed. She becomes a friend and I feel like I'm making connections, finding other people who seem to have survived.

Since we will be living in London for the foreseeable future, we need to find somewhere more practical to live. In the new year, after Ben's first birthday and Christmas, we move into a new house. I am sad to be leaving our treetop flat but relieved to no longer have to carry Ben up two flights of stairs and ready to move into a house with just four steps up to the front door. We have more space and wipeable floors, which are both priorities. We have a small study where we can store Ben's equipment. Ben's room is upstairs and I paint it light blue, put up curtains with giraffes on, and stick a huge caterpillar illustration to the wall above his cot.

The house had to be rewired and redecorated before we could move in so it feels fresh and new, though its bones are Victorian. It starts as a blank slate and we slowly fill it with our things from the flat, our belongings that have been in storage and equipment for Ben. We have his specialist chair to use inside, his buggy for outside and a kit of multicoloured blocks and rolls which we can arrange to support him on the floor. He has a new standing frame that we strap him into so that he is held vertically, arms resting on a tray in front of him. In the kitchen, which is open to the sitting and dining areas, there are medicines, specialist milks and reservoirs to fit inside Ben's feeding pump, and syringes drying on the draining board. I have little control over what is in the house or how it looks. There is so much stuff, everywhere. It's all essential but I don't want us to need it.

When we go to the pub to meet a group of friends we have to remember all of the feeding equipment as well as nappies, spare clothes, cloths. We have now learned how to do this – we only do one thing a day and we pack everything we might possibly need. James and I take it in turns to hold Ben, wearing the backpack with his feeding pump in and trying not to get the tubing running between Ben and the bag caught on anything. We keep a cloth in our hands in case he's sick.

At our new house we position Ben's chair next to us by the sofa so he is able to see the whole room. He is opposite the TV and can also watch me in the kitchen. He looks across to the bookshelves and we start filling a low shelf with his books.

This is closer to what I had imagined my house would be like when I had a child. We settle into the house and our routines. Ben continues to get every cough and cold going but it feels less constant as we come into spring.

I get used to being at work and then James changes job, moving away from government to a human rights organization. In our minds it will be less intense and he won't have to work such long hours. The combination of inflexible, stressful work and the intensity of caring for Ben has been difficult. But James specializes in the Middle East and within days of starting his new job the Arab Spring starts and he's busier than ever. Our lives don't get any more straightforward, or any more relaxed, but we get better at managing what Ben needs. As we begin to appear to others to be parents who have things under control, we start to believe it ourselves.

We begin to work on helping Ben to communicate in the absence of him being able to point or speak. A speech and language therapist suggests we teach him to look instead of point, which is called 'eyegaze pointing', so I buy a menagerie of model animals and we practise him looking to show me where a particular animal is. I hold two toys up in front of him and ask, 'Where is the cow?' Ben learns to look at the cow and then back at me, to show me he is choosing the cow. We play a version of 'I Spy' where he has to identify the object by eyegaze. 'I spy with my little eye: the floor,' I say, and Ben learns to look at the floor. It's simple but shows that he knows words. Through this game he learns the word 'fireplace' before he knows the names for most foods, since he barely eats.

On one of the days that Ben and I are at home together we walk down to the shop and buy James a bar of chocolate. When we return home, I put it on the bookshelf opposite Ben's chair. 'You can show Daddy where his present is when he gets home,' I say to Ben. When James returns in time to put Ben to bed, I tell him Ben has a present for him. 'Do you, Ben? Did you buy me a present?' James asks and Ben stares furiously at the place on the bookshelf where the bar of chocolate is propped up. James follows his gaze and picks it up. 'Thank you, Ben, that's my favourite,' he says as he kisses Ben and Ben grins. These moments are precious.

In the summer, the three of us go on holiday to Scotland. We drive up to Yorkshire, which looks very different to when we left it in the snow, and then continue up through Northumberland to Perthshire. We stay in a small cottage at the end of a track that leads to the moors. Mealtimes are long as we slowly feed Ben with a spoon as well as his tube feeds. We are encouraged by how much thickened yoghurt he is able to eat – not enough to sustain him but still the most he's ever eaten.

Like at home, Ben sleeps badly and the frustration of another night where it's not possible to settle him is just as acute on the moorland as it is in the city. James and I have a fight in the middle of one night because we are all awake, all tired and I hear James talking to Ben abruptly. I feel like he isn't being patient enough, though I know I too have moments of intense irritation during these disrupted nights.

I'm also annoyed to be awake on one of the nights that I'm meant to be able to sleep through, so I shout at James before declaring that I'll take over. By morning we are all friends again and the day is peaceful, though odd because on the fuzzy radio in the cottage we hear about riots close to our house in London.

We get a train from the nearest village into Edinburgh where the festival is on. While James goes to a comedy show, I take Ben to a gallery of modern art. We see an exhibition of Hiroshi Sugimoto's images of photographic plates being electrocuted. They are dark pictures with bright white explosions of light, what he calls 'Lightning Fields'. He seems to have made the invisible visible in all its unpredictable, unique beauty. Perhaps this is what is going on in our bodies – microscopic crackles between synapses and cells that we don't normally see. Maybe we all have little fizzing rivers of energy flowing from our brains to our muscles, but Ben's are more like these bright cracks and unpredictable explosions of activity. I am hoping Ben will let me see the whole exhibition, wary that if he is unsettled or something goes wrong with his milk I don't have James there to help me. But as I push Ben around the museum in his laden buggy he is calm, looking up at the flares of light.

I buy a poster of one of these white lightning bolts frozen mid-strike, with the artist's name in bold text above and the Edinburgh gallery written below. For the next two years, until we move house and the frame gets accidentally smashed, the print hangs above our bed. A little flash of inspiration.

As Ben turns two later that year, the stories we tell him get longer. He is given a copy of *Stick Man* by Julia Donaldson and he likes it. There is a point where Father Christmas is stuck up a chimney. We read it in a deep voice: 'Oh ho ho ho ho, I'm stuck, get me out!' and Ben laughs. I read this book hundreds of times, until I can recite it by heart. If we are waiting for an appointment, or stuck in traffic, I can tell him the story word for word like a personal maternal version of an audiobook. Ben will allow himself to be comforted by these stories. They become familiar and absorbing for us both.

We had started going to Small Steps, a weekly conductive education group run by a charity in west London when Ben was one. It is a mixture of physical, sensory and communication therapy where we are in a group of five children and their parents or carers. It involves two hours' travelling time for a two-hour session but it is worth it for the expertise of the educators and the camaraderie of the other parents. We are taught how to help Ben sit on chairs, supporting him from behind, and how to help him roll down ramps.

One morning, I sit behind Ben on a low stool, holding onto his torso, and help him dip his feet in shaving foam. As we say 'stamp stamp' to him, encouraging him to move his feet, he laughs loudly. He is so small and so radiant that everyone else laughs too. His giggling lights up his whole face and the more we say it, the more he chuckles until he gets hiccups and then reflux. He stops laughing immediately as he grimaces. The teacher looks over and says, 'Oh no, not again,' because this is what happens when he finds something really funny. It is so unfair that moments of fun cause discomfort for him.

At this group I find other mothers who are having similar experiences to me. We discuss physio exercises in the way that other mothers discuss baby-led weaning and swap stories about nurseries and husbands. The educators get to know Ben and are able to suggest how we can help him gain strength and increase his tolerance for different sensations. Some sessions we drip water on him to simulate rain and use a handheld fan to make wind. Another week we put our hands in spaghetti and I give him a tiny taste of a crisp. The variety feels exciting and productive. This is therapy but it is not a chore.

At the end of the sessions we sit around a table chatting and eating. I notice Ben is the only one unable to eat. My comparative internal monologue starts: that child can eat and Ben can't, but that child needs oxygen and Ben doesn't. I feel like Ben is the most severely affected child, as so often happens when we find ourselves in groups of children, but I don't mind because we get so much out of the sessions.

One evening, Small Steps arranges for a woman to talk to parents about stages of grief and how parents of disabled children often experience similar feelings. They may grieve for the way their life is different from their expectations or how their child isn't the child they anticipated. I'm not sure I have followed the exact path she describes and at some level I'm uncomfortable talking about grieving for a child who is very much alive. But I am coming out of a period of feeling sad and overwhelmed, and am becoming more concerned with easing Ben's experience of the world than I am angry about his impairments. If someone gave me a magic wand I would take away his disability, but I'm becoming more focused on what I can do to make his life enjoyable. I'm not spending *every* day upset that he cannot do what I thought he would do. Ben's discomfort is caused by his body's inability to work typically and I hate that this gets in the way of him experiencing joy and pleasure. I can't yet see that there's a difference between wanting to fix Ben and wanting to fix the problems he's experiencing.

It helps to be able to have these kinds of conversations and meet other women in similar situations. My first experience of this had been when I wasn't able to express enough milk for Ben when he was in hospital despite Maddy printing pictures of Ben for me that I could look at while expressing. The feeding nurse, Ellen, had helped me and asked whether I would like to speak to someone who had been in a similar position. She gave me the phone number of Rachel, whose first child was a year or two older than mine.

By the time I met Rachel, Ben was just out of hospital and I had stopped expressing completely. She came round to my parents' house anyway with her son, who still had difficulty eating but was making progress. It was the first time I had met someone who seemed to understand what had happened to me. She talked about how hard the first year of her son's life had been and how lost she had felt. I liked her but I was amazed that she was pregnant again. She was telling me how similar she had felt to the way I was feeling and yet she was now optimistic enough to have another child. She had survived her son's feeding difficulties. Rachel kept telling me how well I was doing and I was touched.

The thought of getting pregnant again was unthinkable to me for a long time after Ben's birth. Occasionally people would ask me if we planned to have more children and I felt panicky just at the thought of it. When I had met women who had gone on to have other babies after their first child was disabled, as Rachel had, I was confused. It was unfathomable. Did they feel ready to risk having another child who could be disabled too? Could they handle two children?

Over the summer in Scotland I realized that I no longer felt terror at the thought of being pregnant again. And now, as Ben turns two, I discover I am expecting another baby. We hope we are through the firefighting stage of our lives and into a period where we will be able to manage two children. We know it will be difficult but we had always planned to have more than one child, and I don't want Ben to miss out on siblings. I want him to have been one of my babies, not my only one.

We are now so used to feeding Ben though his tube it's become unremarkable. My mum, my mother-in-law and Ben's keyworkers at nursery can feed him confidently. It's working well. But the tube in Ben's tummy is discoloured after two years of use and we have to trim the end off it periodically when the plastic splits so it is getting shorter. Occasionally we have given Ben tablet medication which we haven't crushed quite enough and it blocks the narrow channel. This sends us into a panic because the tube is permanent and can only be replaced surgically, under general anaesthetic. We have always managed to unblock it ourselves with a hastily found small syringe but it often happens at the most inopportune of moments.

Ben's tummy is now healed enough for his permanent feeding tube to be replaced with a low-profile 'button' – a little plastic device in his abdomen kept in place by a balloon filled with water within his stomach. Instead of a tube dangling from his tummy all the time, we will connect a temporary tube to the external part of the button when we are feeding him and then remove the tube when we are finished. If the button or tube blocks we can change it at home. We are not looking forward to Ben having another operation and all of the disruption and heartbreak that entails but we are keen to go back to some of the self-reliance we had with the nasogastric tube. If the new button or tube blocks we will be able to change it at home rather than take Ben to the hospital. It will feel weird – poking a plastic device through a hole in my son's torso – but I earned my stripes putting tubes down his nose so I know I'll be able to replace the button when necessary. We have been tucking the permanent tube up into Ben's babygro to stop it getting caught on the edge of a chair or the car seat. We've been cleaning it when it has flicked into his nappy, and checking it's not digging into his back when he's been sitting. As the button will have a removable tube, for the first time since he was born Ben won't have a tube dangling from him all the time. It will be one less thing to worry about.

Ben has the operation to change the tube when I am almost eight months pregnant because we want to do it before the baby is born. It is simple and goes smoothly, though with the hormones of pregnancy I am even more emotional than usual and burst into tears repeatedly at all stages of admission, surgery and recovery.

James stays with Ben overnight because my belly and I barely fit onto the hospital camp bed. The feeding nurse, Ellen, returns to show us how to connect the extension tube to the new button and it is the easiest thing she has taught us so far. We return home the next day and I'm pleased that we have done this when we have only one child, when we can both be fully focused on Ben's recovery. I imagine things are going to be more complicated with a new baby.

The change to a button feels like a little reclaiming of Ben's body. Now, after a bath, when he is lying on a clean towel and I recite *Stick Man* while getting him into his pyjamas, the only sign of Ben's feeding difficulties is a neat little plastic bump on his tummy. It feels so unencumbered. Now that he has lost the chubby rolls of fat on his thighs and the dangling tube, he looks so long and neat with nothing extraneous, not flesh nor plastic.

Ben is still fed milk through his tube, in addition to water and medication. As he has got bigger and as his tolerance to cow's milk has fluctuated the milks have changed, but essentially he is having high-calorie milk pumped through his tube three or four times a day. This works well, in that it's much better than the hand-held gravity syringe feeding of his early months and he is gaining sufficient weight, but he is vomiting a lot due to reflux. In the same way that the muscles that should keep his torso vertical are weak, the tight ring that is meant to stop milk sloshing straight back up from his stomach is loose. What should be a one-way flow is a continuous cycle: we put milk in his tummy and it swooshes straight back up, now made caustic by stomach acid. He has repeated chest infections because the milk has dribbled down into his lungs. The vomiting makes him miserable and visiting anyone with soft furnishings risky. But as far as we are aware we have no other options, so we just make sure Ben is away from the sofa when we give him his dinner (the riskiest meal) and mop up puddles.

It is incredibly hard for Ben to co-ordinate his mouth and tongue to eat or drink. We have been feeding him orally, carefully loading different tastes and textures of purée onto the end of a spoon and placing it at the front of his mouth. He has enjoyed it but the process of using his tongue to move food from the front to the back of his mouth, closing his windpipe and then swallowing the food is not natural to him. He moves his tongue almost continuously but often in the wrong direction and eating is tiring for him. As he has got more teeth he has became increasingly annoyed by any attempts to feed him this way. When he is two he starts whinging as soon as he sees a spoon, before the food even approaches his lips. This is oral aversion, we are told, and we have to be careful that it doesn't get worse. Some children become sensitive to their faces being touched, we hear. I kiss his face even more frequently just in case.

I am surprised by how equanimous we are about Ben's slow but certain refusal to eat. We start offering him food at fewer meals and within a few months we aren't feeding him regularly by mouth at all. We still give him tasters of yoghurt on our finger or hold a piece of mango at the front of his mouth for him to suck, but we don't use any spoons or do it every day. We have known for a long time that Ben wouldn't be able to eat enough to keep himself alive, which is why he has a feeding tube, but we hoped he could at least enjoy the taste and sensation of food. It's increasingly clear that he not only doesn't enjoy it, he actively dislikes eating, and the process of oral feeding becomes an unwelcome chore for us all. So we stop. The time we would have spent feeding him by mouth can be better spent reading books or helping him communicate.

We see an obstetrician throughout my second pregnancy who allays our fears and reassuringly answers our questions. We are worried about problems during the birth and our baby being unwell. She arranges to have a paediatrician present at the birth when we eventually agree on a date for an elective caesarean section. We are nervous but appreciate the calm, methodical nature of a planned birth like this. The caesarean falls on my birthday and will now be my son's too. I am so focused on trying to ensure the success of this birth that it doesn't occur to me to object. All I care about is the good health of our baby.

As we wait in theatre on the morning of the birth, the neonatologist walks into the room. James realizes he knows him, from years before. 'You always know people wherever we go!' I joke to James and we are distracted from our apprehension a tiny bit. When everything is ready, the obstetrician makes her incision and our second baby is born. He is given to me immediately, as I had requested. James helps me hold him up near my face but I'm too nauseous and distracted by the ongoing activity of the obstetrician to have him there for long and James moves him to his chest. The neonatologist and midwife check the baby and have some concerns about his breathing but he is otherwise declared well.

James holds him close while I am stitched up and then all three of us return to the recovery area. We decide his name is Max and tell Maddy when she arrives. I keep Max against my skin and barely let go. I am so relieved to have this tiny baby out of my body safely and to be able to smell and feel him. He is warm and soft, still bunched up in a ball, and I drink in everything about him.

When I give him up briefly, James holds him against his chest and I can see that he is counting Max's breaths. I don't want anything to be wrong so I am almost ignoring everyone's concerns, but James knows something isn't right. He calls his brother Harry, a paediatrician, and speaks to a midwife. She agrees Max needs to be checked, calls a doctor and by mid-afternoon Harry arrives at the hospital. James, Harry and Max go for some tests to check Max's oxygen levels. I remain in the bed, my legs still numb from anaesthetic. I'm worried and feel bereft on my own without the weight and warmth of my baby on my chest.

James returns a little while later, alone, to tell me Max has been admitted to neonatal intensive care (NICU) because he needs help to breathe. I am heartbroken. I had hoped this baby would not be taken away from me on the day he was born, and that we would be able to get to know each other immediately. Like last time, my baby needs more than I can give him. He requires medical expertise and additional oxygen that I can't provide and I'm grateful that he's being treated but devastated we have been separated.

It is evening by the time I am transferred to the postnatal ward. Maddy accompanies me while James is with Max. I want to visit them immediately but I can't yet walk and there is no one to take me there, so Maddy finds a wheelchair and is helping to move me into it from the bed when a healthcare assistant comes over and tells her to leave. 'Visiting hours are finished,' she says, just as Maddy is arranging my bloodstained dressings and my catheter bag of urine on the chair.

'But no one else is helping me and I need to see my baby,' I say. 'Well it can't be her because visiting hours are over,' she says looking at Maddy.

'My baby is in NICU and I need to see him,' I say loudly, despite being surrounded by other women and their babies. 'No one is helping me apart from my sister and I need to get to my baby,' I say tearfully.

'You need to leave us alone,' Maddy says to the healthcare assistant and she walks away as Maddy starts pushing me towards the doors.

It is night-time and everything is quiet apart from the occasional baby's cry. Maddy pulls me backwards, because that is the only way the wheelchair will work, out of the postnatal ward, across the hall and into NICU. James meets us at the doors, concerned that I am already crying, and warns me what to expect before wheeling me through. I haven't seen Max for hours. He is in a room similar to the one that Ben was in two and a half years previously in a different hospital, covered in wires, with a canula in his head and a nasogastric tube on his face. He is surrounded by beeps and nurses just like Ben was. James and I are so sad and shocked, again.

Max is asleep and I cannot hold him so I return to the postnatal ward and try to rest in a bay surrounded by other people's babies. Over the next two days, once my catheter is removed, I walk across to NICU every few hours to sit with Max and express milk, and later to try and breastfeed him. I'm exhausted and resent having to wait in the corridor when there is no one to buzz me into NICU or back into the postnatal ward. I bump into other women doing the same journey and we chat as we wait in the bright, anonymous corridor. 'If you'd taken all your clothes off during labour and run around like me, totally mad, then you'd probably have got your own room,' one woman says.

I don't want to be in a NICU again. I hate all the noises and the worry about whether my baby is going to be OK, but at least I know the drill. I know how to express my colostrum into tiny syringes and then milk, once it comes through, into bottles. I am relieved that this hospital can afford disposable collection sets so I don't have to wash and sterilize the pumping equipment like last time. I am familiar with the systems for lockers and hand washing. We speak the language of neonatal care so we can have efficient conversations with doctors and nurses. When they find out about Ben they are taken aback and apologetic that this is happening to us again, but make sure we realize there is a distinction. 'This is different. They are not the same babies,' the nurses say. A doctor tells us Max is going to be OK and we want to believe him, but it all feels the same as last time.

They are right. Max's breathing improves on day two so he no longer needs supplemental oxygen and we are relieved. This is a much faster recovery than with Ben and they start to feel like different babies. Max improves rapidly and progresses quickly along the rooms off the NICU corridor into Special Care.

On the third day, Ben comes to visit with James's parents and I am so pleased to see him. I am too sore to be able to support his heavy, fidgety body so James holds him next to me and I cradle Max as we introduce them. 'This is your brother,' I say to Ben and he is fairly uninterested until we tell him the names of the things he is looking at in the room. He smiles as I start to read from a book James has brought in and I cry, trying not to interrupt the story. There is so much going on, happy and sad, and I love both of these children almost too much.

The next day, I am told I need to leave the postnatal ward as I am healing well and they need my bed for another woman. There are no other beds for me to stay in and I am upset at the thought of leaving the hospital without my baby. The neonatal ward sister says she can ask to extend my stay for one more night, so that I am close to my baby and can continue to try to breastfeed him. She is kind and gentle and enquires whether I'm getting much sleep. 'Not really,' I say. 'The other babies wake me up and I set an alarm every three hours to come and pump, and I often get woken up by the catering staff for meals I do not want. Also, I have had a headache for three days.' She suggests it might be a good idea to have a night sleeping in my own bed. I reluctantly agree, feeling like she has given me permission to leave the hospital, and although I am intensely sad that my baby is staying, I return home with James. When I wake up the next morning, and take painkillers with a cup of tea as James gets the breast pump ready, my headache has gone. James calls the ward to check on Max, just like we did with Ben, and I dislike how familiar we are with this process of not being in the same place as our baby.

Max now has no wires attached to him except a canula in his hand and is only kept in hospital by his inability to breastfeed. I am trying my best but Max is sleepy and distracted and no amount of scheduled skin-to-skin contact or attempts to breastfeed in the corner of a busy baby unit are working. Everyone, including me, is keen for him to breastfeed but I am keener on us all being at home and I refuse to let feeding be an issue if it doesn't need to be.

James and I suggest to the medical team that we give Max bottles of expressed milk, or formula milk if I don't express enough. Everyone agrees that this is a good plan so James feeds Max a bottle of milk and he drinks it all. Within 24 hours, on Max's sixth day of life, we take him home. Within days Max is happily breastfeeding as well as having formula milk. Max drinking from a bottle feels like a miracle not a failure.

James has six weeks off work after Max is born and it feels like a honeymoon period of us all getting to know Max and adjusting to being a family of four. Ben accommodates the new arrival with little fuss and minimal engagement. He isn't keen on Max crying but he doesn't cry often. A nanny, Rebecca, started part time just before Max was born and this means Ben can carry on doing the therapy and activities he is used to when James returns to work. I have known Rebecca for 20 years — she looked after a friend of Maddy's when we were younger — and I knew she adored children. It was the first time someone else had looked after him at home, but Ben liked her immediately. He laughs at her silly voices and happily sits with her when she does his physio. She hasn't looked after a child exactly like Ben before but has lots of experience of children in general and a willingness to learn.

On the days Rebecca isn't with us, I take Ben to nursery and I'm then alone with Max. With no appointments to go to, there is so much time. I watch a lot of TV and go for walks and revel in the simplicity of this new baby who sleeps and feeds easily. When he wakes in the night I breastfeed him in bed and he almost always goes straight back to sleep. When I leave the house with him I only take some nappies and spare clothes, which feels like nothing. If someone asks me how Max is, I reply, 'He's great. He's happy,' and it's the whole, simple truth.

There are difficult days. James travels to the Middle East for three weeks when Max is four months old and I feel the full weight of responsibility for two children. I struggle through both boys waking up in the night. Once he's back, there are days when I am just holding on until James returns from work. It is difficult looking after Max and Ben on my own for even short periods when they need such different things at the same time but I am totally charmed by them both. I love spending time with them.

As Max grows he doesn't get to go to many of the baby groups because he so often needs to accompany us to Ben's appointments. He gets to play in paediatric gyms while Ben is doing physio. On one occasion, he gets an abscess looked at by a surgeon because he has come along with us to one of Ben's hospital appointments. Rebecca takes Ben to parks and therapy appointments while Max naps at home. Sometimes Max spends the day with Rebecca while I spend time with Ben, taking him to Small Steps or to see friends.

We are relaxed about Max's development and do nothing special to encourage him and yet his progress is staggering. It is bittersweet watching him rolling and holding toys. I later quip that we could have left him watching CBeebies programmes for a year and he still would have walked, but the truth is I am taken aback by the ease with which Max moves and controls his body even at this early stage. I realize that no amount of therapeutic input would have given Ben a body like Max's. No matter how much time I had spent helping Ben roll or sit, he would not have been able to overcome the essential wobbliness and involuntary movement of his muscles. I am relieved rather than sad. I had been worrying whether I had been doing enough for Ben, whether if I was a more devoted mother or a more rigorous pseudo-therapist he would be less disabled, but I now see that this can't possibly be true. Ben's impairments cannot be taken away.

5

Ben loves watching TV. His favourite programme is about a noisy lion called Raa Raa. One afternoon, I put him in his standing frame and, even though he is strapped in from chest to feet, it is hard work for him to keep his head up. He constantly sways from one side to the other, trying to keep his head in the middle to watch the lion. Despite all this effort, he still lets out a little chuckle every time Raa Raa talks about where he lives, in the 'jingly jangly jungle'.

Aged two, Ben is unrecognizable in some ways from when he was a baby. He now has a full head of hair and is much, much taller. When I lift or hold him he feels enormous and solid compared with baby Max. In personality and understanding, Ben is very much a toddler (though not toddling). He has clear views about what he watches – *Raa Raa* or *Rhyme Rocket*, absolutely not *Octonauts* – but in physical ability he hasn't changed much since he was a baby. The way we feed him is the same – through his feeding tube – and the way he moves and controls his body is only slightly different. I resist comparisons between Ben and Max but the boys are similar, needing almost the same level of care and supervision, though in different ways.

I had expected having multiple children to be linear – one child would grow up as another was born behind them. They would move through the years and developmental stages consecutively. Our children will be chronological in age but possibly nothing else. They won't follow each other along a nice straight line, but rather have their own paths that might meander along together or diverge dramatically.

As Ben got heavier, his buggy, so often weighed down with bags, became harder to bump up the stairs to our house. I had bought it when I was pregnant with him, imagining we would need a buggy that wouldn't get crushed by airport luggage handlers. It had turned out to be a robust option given how much we relied on it. My dad never quite got the hang of it, once delivering Ben back to me after a stay at their house saying, 'That f**king buggy is in the car but I had to fold down all the back seats to get it in because it is impossible to pack away.'

Ben slumped in the buggy seat and no amount of tightening the straps could compensate for his tendency to tilt to the side. Our occupational therapist gently talked me through the transition to a more supportive buggy and eventually referred us to the wheelchair service. Just before Max was born, we got Ben's first specialist buggy and so began our ceding of control. The new buggy wasn't one that I picked out at a department store, choosing the colour I liked most or the one that most suited my budget. It was one allocated to us by a wheelchair therapist. I had little control over what it looked like or how it functioned and it felt like it would probably be the first of many decisions that would be taken out of my hands, not necessarily by therapists but by Ben's needs.

Ben is a typical size for a two-year-old so he wasn't given a wheelchair but a version of a buggy that was more supportive. It keeps his wobbly torso straight with a chest strap and lateral supports but we can still take it apart to fit it in the boot of our car. I see the advantages − Ben sits well in it − but I also feel sad that we need this clunky piece of equipment. Rather than the efficient one-handed fold of our previous buggy (provided you weren't my dad), this one pinches our fingers and bashes our calves. It is hard to manoeuvre around our small house and is nothing like the sleek engineering of the buggies we were looking at for Max. It feels like an imposition. I resent its size and appearance.

Using a wheelchair is a sort of shorthand for being disabled − easy to understand, simpler to explain than a dysphagia or cognitive impairment and a good graphic symbol. It is the approachable face of disability. In some ways not so different from the previous buggy, but the new supportive buggy is nevertheless intimidating in its unfamiliarity to me. And yet I know this is what Ben needs − I am not naive enough to think his need for mobility aids is temporary.

When Ben was very small we had been fearful of him not walking but I rarely worry about that now. Ben's daily difficulties with eating and communicating are harder for him and us than his inability to walk. Occasionally someone asks me if Ben will always need a wheelchair and I say, 'Oh, yes' in surprise because I have forgotten anyone might think this was a transitory stage. I have conflicting emotions: I feel intimidated by the reality of a lifetime of wheelchairs for Ben and displeased at others presuming that him needing a wheelchair is bad. Perhaps there is a little whisper of that thought in my own head. I didn't want to admit that I too might prefer he didn't need it, that I feel self-conscious pushing this unwieldy machine around, but I wouldn't speak it out loud.

Luckily Ben and his new buggy are still small enough that we can carry him down flights of stairs and onto boats, into friends' engagement parties and into theatres. Lots of people still carry their two-year-olds occasionally, we just carry him more. I don't have to face all of the implications of him being a wheelchair user yet.

Ben is bothered by bright sun and strong winds, both making him miserable, so I order a hood and rain cover for his specialist buggy at great expense. These accessories are not 'essential' according to the wheelchair service and so not funded by them. As James unpacks them, I am shocked at how crude and impractical they are. I don't want Ben to get wet but I also don't want to need and use these ugly things. I burst into tears. It's not Ben making me sad, it's all the cumbersome stuff which we are forced to deal with. I don't want to have to buy expensive, flimsy specialist items for him only for them to need returning, or spend time having to manage equipment he needs when just looking after him is enough of a challenge. I want to just focus on him, not all of this other stuff which gets in my way.

The task of managing Ben's body is near continuous – he is still sick a lot and now isn't putting on enough weight. I read an article about a way of tube feeding children called Blended Diet, where parents blend food to a milkshake-like consistency and push it through their child's tube. A study claims some children who were fed a blended diet instead of milk had reduced reflux symptoms and vomited less.

I do some research and speak to the doctors and therapists we see. None of them had seen other patients fed in this way. Some are intrigued, others are nervous but no one tells me I shouldn't do it. Some express doubts – it will be harder to calculate the number of calories Ben gets, and there's a risk of blocking the tube or introducing bacteria. But I will soon be weaning Max and it seems to me that weaning a baby and introducing blended diet are comparable. We know Ben is OK with some foods, since he had been eating a little, so if I treat the reintroduction of food to Ben in the same way as I will with Max then the risks must be manageable. When I speak to Ben's dietician she says her professional body are still deciding what the official guidance is but she will support us as much as she can.

I am both relieved and confused by the lack of scrutiny of Max by any health professionals. We see a health visitor occasionally, and doctors for specific issues, but there is only cursory interest in what or how we are feeding him or what he is doing. I am so used to discussing every aspect of Ben's life with numerous people that I now wonder if I have become institutionalized. I see every aspect of Ben's life as needing some form of medical consideration when maybe I should be more confident in what I think is best. I have a kind of clarity in the period immediately following Max's birth, helped by feeling confident about my ability to look after him, where I start to feel empowered to decide what is best for both my children.

When Max is six weeks old, I fill a syringe with fruit and vegetable baby food, tap out the trapped air bubbles, and push the purée through Ben's tube. At the beginning, I do this in addition to his milk feeds and then gradually I start replacing part of the feed. When this goes well, I begin blending my own meals for him. I don't have a good enough blender so I whizz up what I can and then push it through a sieve before drawing it up for him so I'm certain there aren't lumps that will block his tube. It's time consuming but I am determined not to make mistakes and give anyone a reason to tell me I shouldn't be doing it.

When Max is old enough to start eating, I feed him the same pouches of food, though he is keener on gnawing on wedges of fruit. Over months, I introduce meat and fat, carbs and nuts to both of them, and it works. It isn't a magical solution but Ben is sick less. We are reading the book *Avocado Baby* by John Burningham to Ben. Like the mother in the book, who finds feeding her child difficult, I cut an avocado in half, mash it and give it to my child, through a tube rather than on a spoon: 'From that day on an amazing thing happened. The baby became very strong.' I remember this book from when I was little and I love the story of the baby who thrives – defeating burglars and throwing bullies into ponds. The baby gets stronger every day and it's just the kind of outlandish, optimistic story we need.

We are trying to fatten Ben up but if we give him too much food or milk, or too fast, he is sick. Every time he is ill he cannot tolerate food for days, which means he loses weight rapidly and it takes months for him to regain it. The blended diet is not a total fix, but it's an improvement on milk. When he's ill, I blend boiled rice and coconut milk, or toast and banana. When he's recovered, I stave off anaemia with liver and kale, encouraging his growth with olive oil and pasta. I buy a high-speed blender so I can liquidize almost anything to a consistency that suits his tube.

I reclaim my ability to feed my child. After almost three years of feeding Ben to a schedule, in ways that we have been trained to do, I find a way to feed him that feels like I chose it. I like buying bananas in the morning, feeding them to Max at lunchtime (still amazed by the fine motor skills that allow him to pick up the pieces) and then to Ben in the afternoon. Based on little more than my own instinct, I become convinced that it must be best for him to have a variety of food with fresh vegetables and healthy fats. I also reclaim the sound of my life. Rather than the hectoring beeps of a feeding pump, reminiscent of NICU monitors, I introduce the occasional roar of a blender, intrusive but intentional. I also change the aroma of my son and my home – rather than the artificial sweetness of milk out of the packet, making our sink sticky, we smell meat roasting and spinach wilting.

Some dieticians, who are not able to recommend a switch to blended diet, ask me if it's OK if they pass on my email address to other parents while congratulating me on how well Ben looks. It's an absurd situation and I am bemused because I am a rule follower. I'd rather wait in a queue that's going nowhere than risk being seen as pushy. I barely rebelled as a teen. Yet now I seem to be a renegade mother for feeding my child meals that make him less sick. How strange for this, of all things, to be controversial – by making more work for myself and wanting to feed my two children in similar ways despite their differences.

As Ben turns three we are still working on many of the same developmental milestones as ever; meanwhile Max is acquiring new skills every day. When Max is six months old, I put both boys on the floor on their tummies. Ben needs to have his arms propped over a cushion in order to keep his upper body raised. We have been doing this since he was a few months old. Max can prop himself up without any help and he puts his hands on top of each other in front of him. They both look at the programme on the iPad in front of them, though Ben's head frequently flops down and it takes a few moments for him to lift it again. Max's head stays up throughout, effortlessly.

The difference between them, in physical ability, is becoming ever more marked. I knew this was going to happen but it's incongruous and incredible watching our younger child overtake our older child so obviously.

In other areas of Ben's life there has been substantial progress. From a baby that we couldn't put down, Ben will now happily sit in his chair for hours given the right entertainment. We read him Dr Seuss books that he loves, like *Green Eggs and Ham*. He anticipates the lines and then we discover they have iPad versions which he can just about swipe to turn the pages. He sits with the tablet on his tray, listening to the story and it makes him smile. He has a remarkable attention span for books. Ben's new keyworker at nursery, Imogen, buys her own copies of Ben's favourite books and keeps them in a special bag so that she can read to him, and work on language with him, without the books being moved or damaged by the other children. Ben is starting to identify characters or objects in books by looking to show us his answers to questions. Kind friends offer to read to him in pubs, houses, at parties. They read him the books we have brought or books their kids like and Ben is engrossed. Occasionally he will bite his lip, and James or I will nip over to squeeze his cheeks to release his mouth. Sometimes he will flop to one side and we will quickly reposition him upright. Ben will continue looking at the book through these interruptions. The kindest of our friends pretend they don't notice these moments, our continual watching of him, and continue with the arc of the story. No matter the complexity of parenting Ben, stories are universal.

Being Max's mother allows me into conversations that l had felt excluded from. I can now engage in chats about breastfeeding and weaning without needing to explain tube feeding and unco-ordinated swallowing. I can choose whether to talk about Ben or Max or both when someone asks an innocent question about babies and it feels like a privilege. If I only talk about Max I sometimes feel like a fraud, hiding Ben away like a guilty secret or denying his experience, but I also enjoy not having to explain the intricacies to a person who I have just met in the playground. Having such a full experience of feeding babies, almost every which way, allows me a freedom to reveal as much information as I feel comfortable with in that moment. It feels liberating.

Having Max also forces us to do things that most families do but that we had been avoiding, like going to playgrounds, where we discover Ben loves roundabouts. Before, it felt like we were on the fringes of mainstream family life but now we are able to see similarities between Ben and other kids. Part of me wants to rail against the idea that our experience with Ben isn't normal, because who defines normal? But part of me embraces our family now being less unusual. I want a bit of 'normal', whatever that is. Max encourages us into the crowds, into the jumble of parents and children, movement and slides. He fills our house with toys, chaos and noise in a way that Ben hasn't. He brings a different kind of complexity and unpredictability to our family, along with a need for childproofing, which is delightful.

It feels so clear that to be a good parent to Max I need to feed and change him, keep him clean and close, pour affection upon him and stimulate his interests. It is so easy to do, but when I had tried to do the same for baby Ben, I had found it so hard. Ben had needed more than a typical baby yet it was harder for him to communicate what he required and almost impossible for him to take comfort from anything I offered. Now I realize how much was against us both in those early months. I can see how far we have come and I have a kind of admiration for myself. For us both.

I had thought that being a 'good' mother to Ben was inextricable from how much I had done with him, in terms of exercise and stimulation – the more therapy we did, the better mother I was – but now I wonder if that's true. Now I have two children I have to delegate some things, prioritize others, and accept some get ignored. The world doesn't fall apart. Ben doesn't suffer. I give myself a pass to rely on my instinct rather than berate myself for not doing enough physio.

As we get close to Max's first birthday, I choose not to go back to work because the reality of getting two children to nursery or school and me to work is too intimidating. James is often away with his job and Ben's endless appointments and illnesses will be hard to manage if both of us are at an office. Ben's life works better when I go to most of his appointments. I can tell the physio what the neurologist said at the last appointment and remember to chase the nursery about Ben's new chair. I hope I'll be able to expand his vocabulary as we have time to practise eyegaze pointing. But mainly I want to spend more time with my kids. I once saw going to work as a break from being a mother but I now want to be at home and have a break from work. I want to do as much for these boys as I can. The solution to feeling like I have a lot on my plate is to spend more time with my children, not less. Our family may be different to almost all the other families we know, but I'm going to make it work.

Ben has moved along the corridor at nursery into toddler and then pre-school rooms. Cara, a loud Londoner with no time for platitudes, becomes his keyworker after Imogen and fiercely protects Ben. She feeds back to us on the agency workers employed to support him. 'They're not good enough, Jess. I've told Caroline (the manager) they can't work with him.' We start the process of formalizing the support Ben needs at nursery just as he turns three. The nursery had been getting some additional funding from our local authority but it wasn't sufficient for the one-to-one assistance he needed all day. Ben needs help to touch toys and sit on the floor. For the staff to correctly interpret what Ben is communicating with his eyes they need to be sitting right in front of him, focused, not having to keep an eye on three other children. His keyworker has to change him, feed him and give him his medicine. All of this makes him a more expensive child than his more typical classmates and the nursery has been juggling their staff to do it. They need more money to support him properly and we must start thinking about where he is going to go to school. I am intimidated by the process as I suspect it is going to be as onerous as our last big bureaucratic exercise – applying for Disabled Living Allowance.

I try to speak to everyone I can about where might be good for him. We visit four local schools. Two of them are very close, exactly the kind of schools that I had imagined my children would go to, but I can't see Ben there at all. They are just about accessible by wheelchair but don't have facilities for changing. They have lots of pupils with special educational needs but no pupils with Ben's particular challenges. None of their staff has fed a child through a tube or used alternative means of communication to the extent that Ben will need. The third school is mainstream but has some disabled pupils. The special needs co-ordinators at each of the schools are friendly and don't say they can't take Ben but they say it will be challenging for all of us to make it work and I believe them. The thought of my noise-sensitive, stationary son in these boisterous classrooms is alarming.

The fourth school we visit is a special needs school. When we explain Ben's abilities and challenges to the head she is unperturbed. They have children who are tube fed, who need changing and who use all kinds of alternative communication. She teaches children who are sensitive to many different sorts of stimulation and there are only six children in a class. As we walk round, I try not to feel overwhelmed but instead notice how happy the children are and how nuanced the teaching is. The teachers here are skilled at developing communication in children who can't speak. There are staff everywhere, at least three in each classroom, and we walk past the kind of standing frames and walkers that Ben has at home. It is an unprepossessing, scruffy building filled with the kind of expertise and magic I want for Ben's education.

Ben needs a Statement of Special Educational Need (later to be replaced by an Education, Health and Care Plan) and the nursery send off a request. It is an innocuous beginning to what will become an arduous process. The council send us a letter outlining how the following months will go: the reports from each of the professionals working with Ben will be collated and summarized to produce a draft report outlining what support Ben needs to learn. The report will determine which educational setting could meet his needs. We will be sent the report in order to make comments and to put down the name of our preferred school. It will take no longer than four months.

I am warned by other parents that I mustn't wait for the process to work for us. A friend of a friend tells me that, once I have decided which school suits Ben's needs, I should prepare arguments for why the other settings are unsuitable. I am advised to try to build relationships with headteachers directly. 'Check with the head whether they have a place, don't wait for the local authority to do it,' an advisor says when I phone a helpline. I feel unsure. Surely I don't need to be that pushy?

Reports from Ben's physio, occupational therapist and speech and language therapists start arriving. But when I call the council they say they haven't received them and when I speak to Ben's neurologist he says he has not been asked for a report at all. I realize I have to manage the process as best I can so I collate reports and send them to the council officer myself. I check that the reports are up to date and include all of the ways in which Ben will need to be helped to learn. When I phone the council again and again to check on progress I can't get through. I realize that up until now I have had little skirmishes on Ben's behalf, challenging someone's assumptions or thoughtlessness, but this might be our first proper fight. I need to gear up so I can get Ben into the school that will help him learn best. I can't let his potential go unrealized.

After four months, it is late spring and the special needs school tell us they are ready for Ben to start in the autumn. He can do a year of part-time nursery hours there before officially starting school the following year, which is ideal. The nursery and reception children are in the same class at this school. His current nursery staff are doing their best but they are not specialists so it would be best for Ben to start at the school rather than wait another year. But I have heard nothing from the local authority. When I get through to someone I am told the draft statement has not been finalized and Ben will not be moving to the school in the autumn. 'He's not on the list for that school,' I am told. 'But I have spoken to the head and she says he is,' I say, 'and aren't you meant to wait until the statement is agreed before deciding which provision meets his needs?'

'He is at a nursery, even if it's not a specialist one, so other kids will get priority,' they say.

I am incensed that Ben will be made to wait without anyone properly considering his needs. I read the reports reluctantly as they set out his challenges. We try to focus on the positive, and rarely dwell on what Ben can't do, but this process is brutal. The reports state that Ben learns more slowly than other children, that he needs repetition and a particular approach. They list the milestones Ben has missed and the kind of specific input he needs to make progress. They set out how much of his day is spent feeding and changing so he misses time for play and development. Everyone has tried to be encouraging and complimentary about him but the documents are stark about what Ben can't do or needs help with. 'Ben requires specialist input for communication, movement, posture, feeding and sleeping,' I read, which basically means he needs help with everything.

Nine months after the process began, it's early summer and I am reaching the end of my tether. I arrange to meet with the Special Educational Needs (SEN) department of our local authority to negotiate, and hopefully finalize, Ben's statement. It is on a day where we only have childcare for Max (one of our challenges being that we can't ask anyone to look after Ben and Max at the same time) and Ben has physio just before the meeting so I bring him with me to the council building. I find a disabled parking space and unload Ben, filled with foreboding. If this goes badly he won't be able to start school in September and we will have lost a year of opportunity for him.

When we arrive, the receptionist takes my name and glances at Ben before saying, 'Children are not allowed in any of the meeting rooms.' 'But he can't be disruptive,' I say. 'He can't walk.' 'It's policy,' the receptionist says. James arrives and tries to explain to the receptionist that Ben can't leave his buggy and we have a meeting about him, but they are adamant that Ben cannot enter any rooms. When the head of SEN arrives with a council lawyer she too is unable to overcome the directive and so we hold our meeting around a table in the bustling foyer of the council offices surrounded by visitors and cleaners sweeping the floors.

We start to discuss my comments on the draft statement. I have included recommendations from the therapy reports that had been left out and I have footnoted every single one. The document is ten pages long and is a relentless argument as to why Ben needs the kind of specialist setting that we have requested. We take turns to highlight a particular line or paragraph – about the importance of daily stretching or specialist speech and language therapy. We talk about seating, standing frames and communication devices while James reads books to Ben and finds programmes for him to watch while also attempting to contribute to the conversation. I have never been more familiar with every single line and paragraph in a document.

One of the books James reads to Ben that day is *Iggy Peck Architect*. I had thought I could explain my profession to the kids with this book about a boy who builds 'churches and chapels from peaches and apples, and temples from modelling clay'. We reach the end of the meeting and the head of SEN has agreed to almost all of my comments. She confirms Ben will be put on the list for the special needs school. 'He can start part time in September if that's OK with the headteacher,' she says and I breathe a sigh of relief while not letting my facade of ferocious professionalism slip. 'Are you a lawyer?' she asks. 'No, I'm an architect,' I say, as James finishes the tale of Iggy Peck and I realize that my developing skills of negotiating with local authorities are substantially more use to Ben right now than my ability to design buildings. I'm surprised that I have educated myself sufficiently, and projected enough bravado, to be mistaken for a lawyer, but I hope that Ben has been listening to the book and not our discussion. He can start at the school in less than eight weeks' time. We have won this battle.

6

'Shall I read to you, Ben?' George asks. We are at the beach, on holiday in Spain. It is a glorious sunny day. Maddy and her boyfriend George have joined us, as they do on so many trips. It's their holiday but it also involves them helping us with our children, a lot.

The beach isn't a great environment for Ben. We have dragged his wheelchair through the sand and placed it between our sun loungers, under the shade of an umbrella. We have prepared his lunch and have it ready for him in a cool bag. We'll try taking him into the sea but it will probably be too cold for him to enjoy it, and holding him upright so he can just dip his toes is already a bit back-breaking for me. There are other three-year-olds around us, building sandcastles and licking ice creams, but Ben hates the feeling of sand. He's getting bored, making whiney noises, and so George offers to read to him. 'I don't know where your book is, so let's have a look at this,' he says as he picks up a newspaper. He goes to the football results in the sports section and reads them out to Ben in a funny voice. Ben places his closed fist on George's arm and smirks as George works his way down the page in a variety of voices. James and I take the opportunity to go for a swim. By the time we return they are halfway through the sports section.

We have a lovely, if tiring, holiday. I am still adjusting to holidays with kids that do not really feel like a break. Before we arrived I had contacted the owner of the house we were renting to check the wheelchair access. He told me there were three steps down to the front door. 'But don't worry,' he said, 'I'll make a ramp.' I didn't hear any more but as we arrived at the house, exhausted from our journey, we saw that he had built a ramp covered in black rubber over the steps so we could wheel Ben in and out easily. I was so touched.

On the first night in Spain we tried putting the boys in the same room for the first time, but after hours of them each disturbing the other we gave up and put Max's cot in a bathroom. It means Maddy and George have to go downstairs to the loo but that is better than none of us getting any sleep.

On the way back to London we are waiting at the airport, giving Ben his lunch though his tube, when a lady approaches Ben and Max, who are side by side in their wheelchair and buggy. She starts talking to Ben (ignoring Max) and then me, introducing herself and talking about where she has been. She is American and about to return to the United States. 'What's wrong with him?' she asks me, above Ben's head.

'There's nothing wrong with him. He is disabled,' I say. 'I think we need to go.' I make a great show of checking the departure board and packing up our things, glancing meaningfully at James, who hasn't heard what she has said. 'I'll pray for you,' the lady says loudly. 'There's really no need,' I reply briskly.

A week after we return to London, we move house for the third time since Ben's birth. Our lovely little house, with its stone floors and narrow bathroom, has become increasingly impractical. It's difficult to bump Ben in his specialist buggy, now he is three, up even the short flight of steps to the front door and his equipment has taken over the ground floor. It doesn't have a bath and Ben hates showers. We had started a legal process on Ben's behalf, connected to the medical treatment he received at the time of his birth, and have received a payment which enables us to rent a bigger house. With some sadness but a determination to do what's necessary, we move half a mile down the hill.

The new house has an accommodating landlord, no steps up to the front door, a large bath and one more bedroom. There is a step down to the kitchen but our carpenter friend Dan comes to build a ramp so Ben can roll down. The house has wide back doors that open onto a garden filled with plants and when we move in, at the height of the summer, the passion flower is in full bloom and there are grapes hanging from the vines. Ben can no longer live in a home like our first flat in the treetops, but this house has some of the feel of it – white walls and grey floors, a calm backdrop to the constant chaos of our family life. We're no longer at the height of the tree canopy but down at the level of the soil and at this time of the year the garden is abundant. There is a mosque at the end of our garden and, while it doesn't broadcast the call to prayer, it feels like we've come full circle in some way, back to a little of our time in the Middle East when I was pregnant with Ben. We now have the space to buy Ben a swing and he happily sways in the shadow of the mosque – he is now too big to be swayed in our arms, but small enough to fit into a moulded seat of a swing and have his feet brush the tall grass.

Ben is accommodating of the move and doesn't mind having a new bedroom. Max is discombobulated. He is 15 months old and potters around the house confused about where his toys are and why everything is different. He doesn't like it and though he can't speak he makes his views clear.

A few days after the house move, Ben starts school. He settles in quickly and we feel vindicated that this is the right place for him. I don't need to train anyone or explain how to handle his body. Ben's needs aren't unusual at this school and, once I have explained his routine and what he likes and dislikes, they don't require me to stay. Within days he is happy and loves his teacher who is newly qualified but empathetic, fun and skilled.

We have gradually decreased the amount of milk we give Ben and increased the volume of blended food, and his reflux has improved. Each day that he goes to school we take in his packed lunch – pre-filled syringes of lunch purée. On one level it feels like a shame that he is no longer surrounded by non-disabled peers, but leaving him at school also feels right and strangely simple. I'm much less involved than I was at nursery because his days at school are so straightforward.

Max and I pick him up each day and I treasure every snippet of information: 'Ben joined the choir today'; 'He's been trampolining'; 'Here's a book to read with him at home'. Ben can't tell me about his day so I glean as much as I can from these brief conversations and the notebook they send home with him.

It takes time for me to get used to seeing so many children with impairments, to the noise, unpredictability and number of wheelchairs. It feels bittersweet that Ben belongs here, with children who look and act differently to the children I am used to. Seeing him in this context makes me feel like I'm seeing him objectively, or at least less subjectively. He needs what this school offers. I no longer have to be everything to him.

When we drop Ben off each morning, the headteacher stands at the door greeting each child. Max is 18 months old and can now slip away from me in a way that Ben has never been able to and he waddles into Ben's classroom happily, back against the wall when a child comes past using a walking frame. All of the staff say hello to Max and he is at ease in the school. I admire how easily he accepts how different all the children look. Over the course of the first year, the school comes to feel like somewhere we belong. Ben goes three days a week and we are all looking forward to him being there full time the following year.

A nanny called Christina started working for us earlier that year. Ariving at 7am most mornings, she makes Ben's breakfast while we get up and then looks after Max some days while I drive Ben to school or take him to appointments. Christina is quiet, gentle and very capable. Max loves her and she is friendly to Ben, interested in what he likes and how to engage with him. She asks pertinent questions about how we would like her to look after our children which take me by surprise. When Max empties all of the plastic cups and plates off the shelves in our kitchen she asks me how I would like her to handle it. 'Do you want me to tell him off?' she asks as I step over the mess on the floor to get Ben's lunch. 'Oh no,' I say. I love the novelty of having a child who can walk up to a shelf and pull things off it. I want him to explore more, not less.

Having Christina there means I have a few hours to myself each week, which I treasure. Earlier in the year I started an inclusion training course run by parents of disabled children and disabled people. I didn't really know what it would involve but with a desire to learn I signed up. At the course I hear about the history of disability politics and meet women who have older disabled children. We have training days run by experts, some disabled, and small group sessions where we discuss our lives. I have the youngest child in the group and I feel like I'm a naive creature opening my eyes and ears for the first time. I know a lot about my son but almost nothing about the wider context of issues faced by disabled people.

I learn that disabled people have rewritten the definition of disability: *'Disability is the loss or limitation of the ability to take part in the normal life of the community, due to physical and social barriers.'* Activists have turned the whole thing on its head –

rather than being defined by what they were told they were unable to do, they have self-defined as being disabled by the world around them not letting them participate in the way they would like. The barriers to disabled people living full, unhindered lives are physical (inaccessible buildings) or to do with prejudiced attitudes (assuming disabled people can't work) and discriminatory institutions. This is a revelation to me and makes me think differently about Ben, what he can do and how we deal with it. It gives me the confidence to publicly describe him as disabled.

At the course I find out about the social model of disability which makes a distinction between impairment (for example, Ben's inability to walk) and disability (the restriction he experiences faced with a flight of steps), versus the medical model which sees a disabled person as someone (or a collection of issues) to be fixed, concentrating on what is wrong with them. We talk about the difference between a medical model of individualism – each person's impairment is their problem alone – and a social model that sees communality in the way people are treated and their experiences.

I realize that, only three years into my experience of having Ben, I am becoming conditioned to think that Ben is the problem when faced with inaccessibility of all kinds. I see his wheelchair as the issue rather than the building or the attitude of the people running the building when we can't get up steps. When moving around a place is difficult I start to think it's easier to stay at home. This starts a cycle that I can feel us falling into, where Ben is less visible because he doesn't go out as much and this reinforces a sense of unfamiliarity, that disabled people have no right to be in some spaces and shouldn't be spoken about or included. I realize these cycles of exclusion have been going round and round for centuries and we're just one of the latest families to be experiencing the effects.

The day-to-day manifestations of exclusion can feel trivial. The cumulative effect is insidious. When we're out some people assume Ben can't understand and so don't include him in conversations or activities. We have to ask for special favours and extra help to get through a crowd to the one wheelchair spot. We are almost late for an appointment because the lifts are full of people who could walk up the stairs. We can't get on the train because there isn't a ramp or a space. Because he can't initiate conversations or play, Ben doesn't make conventional friendships with peers and doesn't get invited to birthday parties. Ben can't go to the local school because they don't have appropriate facilities. He can't go to the theatre because they don't have a lift. So it goes on in tiny and massive ways until disabled people aren't taking part in life around them in the way they could be and are effectively segregated. Or disabled people do manage to take part but are exhausted by all the work they have had to do to get themselves where they need or want to be. I realize I'm going to have to fight to keep us on the main track of life – the path with all our friends and neighbours where all the fun and activity is.

When Ben starts in the reception class at school a year later, a face full of freckles after a summer holiday in Cornwall, we are offered transport because the school isn't local. A bus can come and collect him every morning and drop him back every afternoon. I had been driving him to and from school in the nursery year and I have liked being so involved, but I can see the advantage of not spending two hours each day on school runs. James has been travelling a lot with work, and mornings are more hectic when I'm on my own. I decide I will do some drop-offs and pick-ups, so Ben isn't on the bus for every journey and I will still see his teachers. I come up with an elaborate rota, which is confusing for everyone, and after a few weeks we decide Ben will just get the bus every morning.

On the first morning we are waiting at our front window. A big white bus appears outside the house, almost blocking our narrow street. There are already some kids on the bus and they will pick up more after Ben. The driver gets out to greet us with a broad smile. He lifts Ben's wheelchair into the back of the bus and we wait on the pavement for the chair to be strapped in before we wave goodbye. Ben is relaxed but I find it overwhelming. It's a bus full of disabled children and unfamiliar adults and my son is going to join them, to be driven on a route I don't know, without me. We don't know any other children that get a special bus. I always imagined I would walk my children to school and I feel like I'm not just losing control of Ben's world but I'm thrusting him out there, undefended.

However, the driver is relentlessly friendly and the two ladies who are the bus escorts are efficient and smiley with Ben. The whole arrangement is objectively ideal. Ben is fine for the first three days while I come around to the idea. On the fourth day, Ben smiles in response to the driver's broad grin as we walk out of the house but then his bottom lip appears – sticking further out in direct correlation to the ascension of the wheelchair lift. By the time they are strapping his chair in he is crying and won't open his eyes to say goodbye. 'Ben's very sad,' says two-year-old Max. This carries on for a week or two: Ben smiles at the driver when he arrives, gets progressively sadder as he gets into the bus and then cries as the bus leaves. He'll allow himself to open his eyes a little and retract his lip a bit if the bus escorts sing to him but as soon as they stop his tears resume. When I call school mid-morning they say he is not upset. When I see the headteacher she says Ben is happy when he arrives at school. The bus staff say he stops crying as soon as they turn the corner away from home. I think it's just something we all need time to get used to but it makes my heartstrings taut. I feel like we're doing the right thing but I'm unsettled at him leaving me so sad every morning.

Some mornings, a driver stuck behind the bus gets angry, shouting and beeping their horn. I approach them calmly and thank them effusively for waiting. 'It won't be long,' I say. 'We're just getting my disabled son, in his wheelchair, into the bus so he can go to his specialist school.' They are apologetic, they didn't realize they were beeping at a child in a wheelchair, and I take satisfaction in making them feel bad for just a moment.

Each Wednesday, I drive Ben and Max to the school and they have a 30-minute trampolining lesson before Ben's school day starts. In the same way that when he was a baby

Ben craved movements that were strong and firm, being held tight and swung high, he now likes to be bounced as high as we dare. When I lay Ben on the trampoline the instructor bounces around him, getting closer and closer, until his body is being thrown clean of the trampoline. As he is flung around he laughs and shrieks with excitement. When Max is feeling brave he lies nearby and the two of them are bounced in unison, Max's body unable to fully give in to the rebound, not able to fully collapse as Ben's does.

Every afternoon, we pick Ben up from school and Max tells him about his day in toddler speak, a stream of consciousness that Ben isn't that interested in. One afternoon, they are watching *Peppa Pig* at home and Max tries to hold Ben's hand but he can't keep it still. As Ben's hand fiddles around involuntarily, Max tries to hold onto it absent-mindedly, while watching the programme. Ben's arm moves more wildly and he breaks free of Max's grasp. Ben's arm is in front of Max but it soon veers left and he bashes the side of Max's arm, occasionally tapping Max on the head, but Max ignores it entirely. He is so used to his brother's movements, his arms in motion and his accidental swipes and knocks, that I don't think he even notices, until James says, 'Max, is Ben's hand touching you?' and Max looks up, glances at Ben, smiles, waves his arms around in an impression of Ben and returns to watching the programme.

We are constantly discussing every aspect of Ben's life from the relatively straightforward (what we should be feeding him) through to the specialist (what drugs he should be on). It's difficult to know what we should be doing, who he should be seeing, for the best. My tendency since his birth has been to see more people rather than fewer in the hope that we won't miss an opportunity, that we are taking every chance for him to develop. I have equated good mothering with activity. It has been easy to do because there has been no shortage of therapists to see or activities to practise. In the early days, Ben was so miserable much of the time I wanted to try anything that might make him happier.

The inclusion course has made me question how much of what Ben does and how many of the people he sees now are essential. Am I trying to solve his disability? I try to disentangle how much I am treating Ben's impairments as problems to be fixed and how much I am trying to improve his day-to-day life. Over the 18 months of the course I learn how to be an ally to Ben – to facilitate what I think he wants and needs, rather than what I want for him or what I think will make him fit in better. I think back to introducing blended diet – which was not suggested to me by medical professionals – and how that led to Ben having fewer chest infections, better immunity and looking less wan, which made him happier. I did what was right for Ben rather than what was thought to be right for 'children like him'.

I have to start rethinking some of the ways we have been parenting Ben. I have had a simmering resentment towards James for not proactively doing the therapy we have been shown. I feel like James spends more time relaxing with Ben on the sofa at the weekend watching sport than he does doing the physio exercises that would improve Ben's head control. It annoys me because I'm always the one to initiate the therapy, remind James what we're meant to be doing, nagging. Now I start to think that maybe the cuddles on the sofa are the most important of all the interventions. What would Ben rather do? Physio exercises or be nestled with his dad? Which will he be more grateful for in ten years' time? I don't make radical changes – we still take Ben to see a private physio weekly and I drive him to music therapy every Tuesday after school – but my mindset begins to shift.

Between his fourth and fifth birthdays, Ben is seen by nineteen different professionals or clinics (therapists, various hospital consultants, a community doctor, nurses, a dietician, a social worker, etc) which is what we have been doing every year since he was born. Some of them, like hospital clinics, we visit annually or every six months. Some therapists we see weekly, so over the course of the year he has over 150 separate appointments. Many are at home, school or nursery, but I am there for the vast majority of them. Most are with knowledgeable people who we enjoy seeing, but still that's a lot of time each week which isn't spent just hanging out with Ben, doing things he enjoys, doing the kind of mothering I thought I would be doing. And Ben gets no choice about whether he wants these appointments.

Ben's diary is hard to manage logistically, but also emotionally. We encounter a lot of people in various fields at these appointments or when negotiating to get Ben what he needs. I have to hear and read things I would prefer not to. The reports written during the process of getting Ben into his school were primarily focused on what he couldn't do and when I phoned one potential school they said, 'We don't have the luxury of being able to take children as disabled as Ben.' I have to keep hassling an equipment company to get them to deliver a medical bed for Ben which I know we need but am also dreading arriving, in all its clunky, inelegant glory. I am often involved in protracted, energy-sapping bureaucratic ordeals and through it all we are not getting enough sleep and James is travelling frequently for work.

On any given day it's likely that I've been up during the night, even though James and I share the wake-ups between us, and that inevitably affects the quality of my parenting and my resilience. I am less patient with Ben and less tolerant of people saying unwelcome things. The likelihood of me bursting into tears is directly proportional to how tired I am so there is a lot of weeping some weeks. I try to keep it together during difficult appointments but when Ben has been unwell and I don't know how to help him recover, I can't. One afternoon, I find myself in an appointment sitting on a chair crying, with Ben, who has been coughing for a week, in my arms, as a doctor crouches on the floor in front of me. He wipes my tears before sending us to a hospital for tests.

Some of the appointments we have are not urgent but involve reviewing every aspect of Ben's life, so our choices as parents are laid bare and discussed. If they are with professionals who we trust and have a rapport with, they are helpful, but sometimes we have to challenge someone's opinion and I am becoming more confident in my protection of Ben. I start to refuse to let anyone take his blood without them first applying anaesthetic cream. I question whether each test is necessary – will the results help Ben? I cancel appointments that aren't crucial and reschedule others so he won't miss school. I start to refuse to summarize his birth and the first years of Ben's life, a story that I have now retold dozens, if not a hundred, times for professionals. 'It's all in his file,' I say, and if we are at the hospital I glance towards the paper file, which sits ten centimetres tall on the desk and is bursting at the seams.

So much of what is difficult about the dozens of appointments isn't actually about Ben. At my course we discuss the need for professionals to work with their head and their heart. The best people we see are very skilled at what they do and understand something of what our lives are like. They respect our knowledge as parents. They explain options to us and set out our choices or arrange joint visits with other professionals. An occupational therapist talked gently about a wheelchair before we got to that point so I had been prepared. She encouraged us as we helped Ben learn to eye point to make choices, and then mentioned the possibility of eyegaze technology, where he could control a computer with his eyes, a year before she referred us to an assistive technology team. This meant we were ready and not intimidated by new developments. This wasn't by chance – she knew that sowing the seeds of these ideas would make them less intimidating to me and help me realize what Ben's options were.

There are lots of examples of proactive professionals: a physio suggests she comes to a wheelchair appointment with us so she can help explain Ben's posture rather than me having to do it all. A doctor gives me his email address so I can check medication doses without returning to the hospital. These skilled professionals are also the ones that ask about Max because they appreciate that Ben is part of a family and we are parents to two children. They know that every person, especially a disabled child, has a context. The people who surround them, and how they are, are often as important as their own health, or at least have a profound impact upon it.

The irritating professionals we see come to work with only their head and see their interaction with us as a task to tick off in their day. They have limited empathy and see only one aspect of Ben's life, and offer unhelpful, unrealistic suggestions. They make Ben go for an appointment, missing school, because he is a name on their caseload not because they can offer anything to improve his wellbeing, and they expect me to tell them important developments because they haven't read his file. They talk in front of Ben in a way that shows they do not think he can understand.

Some professionals make more work for me rather than less – I get a call one afternoon from a community nurse telling me she is coming round that afternoon because she is concerned about Ben's tummy. I gather, eventually, that the school nurse had called her saying the area around his feeding tube looked sore. I explain to the nurse that we have plans that afternoon and I will be with both children on my own. I tell her that Ben is recovering from an infection, that we are just finishing a course of antibiotics and the soreness is improving. I say I have it in hand. I call the school nurse and email Ben's teacher. If someone had called me initially I could have saved myself, and all of these people, time and effort. The nurse who is suddenly so keen to visit is the same nurse who has never been able to help when Ben's tube site has been sore previously. She doesn't know anything about this latest infection because I had realized during previous episodes that the only way to deal with problems of this type is to bypass her.

I notice people making assumptions about Ben, assuming he can't do things or won't understand. Now I start to have a context for this kind of thinking. I see our family within a society that consistently undervalues disabled people and sees them as individuals who need to be helped or improved. Ben has day-to-day problems which we want to fix, or minimize, to improve his quality of life, but I start to see that he isn't someone we are trying to fix, even if we could. We need to mitigate the inconveniences of his impairments: if we're going to have 150 appointments a year, we can't be dealing with people who offer no value to Ben. He isn't the problem, all the other stuff is. We can embrace the ways Ben is different.

That Christmas, I copy an idea I have seen online for Ben's advent calendar. In previous years we have had paper calendars with opening doors that Ben hasn't been very interested in or wooden calendars which involve me finding 24 small gifts to put in little boxes. Ben's enthusiasm is not sufficient for the effort involved. This year, I buy 24 books, mostly second-hand from charity shops, and wrap them in brown paper. I put a big number on each and stand them up on our shelves. Each day, Ben points, with his eyes, to that day's date. We unwrap the book just in front of him so he can feel the paper if not pull it off and read that day's new book. It becomes an annual tradition and an example of how Ben's differences force us to innovate. He loves books and I enjoy finding them. I like searching for new stories and characters that we can then discover together. The book calendar becomes a precious ritual.

7

Ben loves watching videos of Michael Rosen performing his poems. He likes the way Michael Rosen bulges his eyes as he talks and gesticulates enthusiastically. Ben has always loved gesticulation – when he was younger a friend's mum had been telling us a dreadful story about an accident and as she used her arms to illustrate the magnitude of the horror, Ben giggled at her. 'Sorry,' we said. 'He thinks it's funny when people wave their arms a lot.'

Ben watches these videos hundreds of times while I put on washing and send emails chasing appointments. We already like Michael Rosen's books – *Little Rabbit Foo Foo* was a staple of Ben's early years and we've adapted it into a family skit where we introduce TV characters into the story: 'Little Rabbit Foo Foo riding through the forest, scooping up Mike the Knight and bopping him on the head!' At a Christmas gathering, my mother-in-law, Prudence, and Ben's uncle Harry perform a version of Foo Foo for Ben, which he chuckles at.

We found the Michael Rosen videos through Rik Mayall. Prudence had found an old *Jackanory* episode from 1986 in which Rik Mayall read Roald Dahl's *George's Marvellous Medicine* with his highly expressive face and funny voices. Ben loved it. We all did – after a few years of back-to-back anthropomorphized pigs and lions it was a relief to have Mayall's impression of a sinister granny on in the background. Ben watched it repeatedly, laughed frequently and sometimes shouted loudly in excitement. When he had got bored of it we'd found Michael Rosen's videos as an alternative.

Ben particularly likes one of Michael Rosen's videos about bending a toothbrush when he should have been cleaning his teeth as a kid: 'Bendy bendy bendy, Bendee bendee – CRACK!' His mum says not to worry but his dad works out that he broke the toothbrush and remembers it, so then every time Michael does a 'BAD THING' his dad reminds him of it. 'It's like he had written it down in a book. Michael's BIG BOOK OF BAD THINGS.' Every time Ben watches this video we all laugh.

I discover that Michael Rosen will be performing poems from this book in London and decide we should go. They recommend the show for ages six to nine. Ben is almost five but I know he has the attention span. He just needs to be able to cope with the surroundings. It is a risk. We've had mixed success with theatre trips, or really any big occasions involving noise.

It's hard to work out what combination of drama and music is all right for Ben and what is unacceptable. He'll happily watch Prudence perform a mini-play and go to the story time at a local museum, laughing loudest and longest at a tale of how the elephant got his trunk. He enjoys a kids' music group, smiling at nursery rhymes he recognizes, but when we sang 'Happy Birthday' to him on his fourth birthday Ben stuck out his bottom lip, like he had with every rendition of the song thus far in his life, and cried. As his face crumpled, all of our shocked 'Oh Nos' did not help. I kissed him and my mum started reading a book to him to help him recover. We don't know why this happens but guess that it's some kind of sensory or emotional overload.

Ben has enjoyed productions by Oily Cart, a company that make inventive and brilliant theatre shows specifically for disabled children. He has recently started enjoying going to the cinema. But nine months previously I had taken Ben to a production of *Not Now, Bernard* at a children's theatre and it had been disastrous. It was based on the book where every time Bernard tries to say something to his parents they reply with 'Not now, Bernard' until eventually he is eaten by a monster. I had prepared for the trip by reading the book to Ben numerous times and we'd had a wheelchair spot reserved.

The show started – a man came onto the bright stage just in front of us and I could see Ben tense up. I moved him out of his wheelchair and onto my lap so I could better comfort him but the actor made some loud noises, Ben startled and he burst into tears. I couldn't calm him down so I decided we should leave. Unfortunately, our proximity to the 'stage' (a painted section of the floor) meant I had to carry a sobbing four-year-old, two coats and a bag while pushing a wheelchair onto the stage to get out, thereby causing maximum fuss and creating some inadvertent audience participation. I went straight back to the car where Ben stopped crying but I started. I wanted to take Ben to performances because he so obviously enjoyed stories and theatrics at home. I wanted to give him the joy of seeing live performances, but new experiences were so often disastrous and miserable.

As the date of the Michael Rosen performance nears, James and I agree we will take him together. We arrange to drop Max off with Harry because an unpredictable two-year-old will not help ensure success. We spend a lot of time telling Ben where we are going. So much, in fact, that when anyone says, 'Big Book of …' Max shouts, 'BAD THINGS!' at us all. Ben thinks that's amusing which is a good start.

Our seats are right at the back of the theatre (good) and at some distance from the stage (promising) and we are let into the auditorium first so we watch everyone else come in. Ben has time to get used to the theatre gradually getting busier and noisier. James continuously reads him poems from the Big Book while we wait. Then the lights dim and Michael Rosen comes on stage. As he speaks loudly into his microphone for the first time, James and I hold our breath, watching Ben and waiting. His hands lift a little, a mini startle, when there is a sudden shout. James and I are on tenterhooks but Ben is focused and taut with anticipation rather than anxiety.

As the performance continues, James puts his hand in front of Ben's legs to stop him kicking the chair in front. Michael Rosen performs a familiar bit about getting ready for bed:

'Quick! Wash my face. Clean my teeth…Hey, the toothbrush is a bit wobbleee.'

Ben is totally focused on listening, working hard to keep his head up throughout, but he smiles. As Michael Rosen tells stories involving sudden noises – 'CRACK!' – and one about the Stone Age with loud audience participation, Ben copes. James and I laugh at the jokes but are poised for a flicker of Ben's pursed lip and the pushing back of his upper body which will mean he is getting overwhelmed. It never comes. He handles the sudden, startling noises and it is brilliant. At the end of an hour, Ben is hot with the effort of concentration and tension, but amused.

When it finishes we go to get our book signed and as Michael Rosen walks past he stops to say hello to Ben, 'You seemed to be enjoying that, didn't you?' As we wait in the queue, Ben is squashed between older kids and occasionally involuntarily kicks a child in front of us. They turn, notice the wheelchair and decide not to mind. As we reach the front of the queue, Michael Rosen signs our book: 'Hello Ben! Michael Rosen was here!' Ben is tense after the performance and the queueing but he stares determinedly at his book and Michael Rosen and when we show him the book later, away from the crowds, he smiles broadly. We are finding ways of pushing ourselves out into the world and making it work for Ben. It fills us with a sense of possibility.

Ben goes from watching a performance to being in one with his first school Christmas show – 'Cosmic Christmas'. It isn't a typical nativity play – the pupils are aliens from different planets describing parts of the Christmas story. Each class works with the talents and adjusts to the impairments of pupils in the group. As we arrive and take our seats we are nervous to see how Ben will cope with the occasion.

As part of the performance, they have pre-recorded videos that are projected above the stage. In his class's segment, we watch a film of Ben and another boy smiling as the sun rises on red planet: news has spread that Mary and Joseph are going to Bethlehem. The boys have a subtitled conversation in the film, Ben's lines delivered by him pressing a communication button that has a pre-recorded voice:

Joe: Have you heard?!

Ben: The star said that Mary is having a baby!

Joe: They're crossing the desert to Bethlehem.

It's an ingenious way of delivering the story without putting pressure on the boys to speak or press buttons in the middle of the performance.

The aliens then celebrate with a dance, to African music, their wheelchairs decorated in red. Ben is engaged and quiet. We can see that he is tense – his face tight, his head turning to the right – and we are worried. Ben doesn't smile once but he doesn't cry either. At the end, everyone sings the school song 'Something Inside So Strong' and all of the staff sign the words with their hands as they sing. It is a glorious mix of total chaos (the kids are not still or quiet), festive fun and emotion.

A crew from BBC News is filming the play and they put a video online later that day with the headline: 'The parents who never expected to see their child in a nativity play'. It gets picked up by BBC 5 Live radio and the school asks if I will be interviewed. When a radio producer calls me to discuss the piece he asks, hopefully, 'Did you ever think you'd see your son in a nativity play?' I want to celebrate the school and the kids but it isn't true that we never imagined Ben would take part in a school play. I had never given it much thought, but I didn't feel I had witnessed a Christmas miracle. Ben's school works towards their pupils doing all the things that schools do, which includes performances and involving parents. So I say, 'I hadn't thought about whether I would see him in a play. It was brilliant but loads of good things have happened at school this year.' I tell the producer about Ben's recent progress with simple spelling using an eyegaze computer in his classroom. Ben had come home with a message from his teacher: 'I asked Ben to spell some three-letter words today and he did so no problem!' When I speak live to the presenter a few minutes later I am enthusiastic about the play while gently pushing back on the idea that it was miraculous that disabled children can be part of a play, and at the end the presenter brings up Ben's recent spelling triumph.

The deputy head calls when the segment has finished to say Ben had been listening in his classroom and smiled at my voice. When I go to collect him that afternoon I feel like a minor celebrity. People love a feel-good story about kids and the video is 'most watched' on the BBC website for a good few hours. I am pleased to have been able to publicly recognize the school and all the staff and pupils who worked hard on the play. When I had watched the play, I had been thrilled to see my first child in a performance, anxiously scanning his body for the first hint of a bottom lip or a frenzy of kicking legs, and relieved that he had lasted without finding it overwhelming, but it hadn't occurred to me that I shouldn't have expected to see him in a nativity play.

With Ben settled at school, Rebecca and Christina helping us at home and Ben's reflux symptoms improving, our days with Ben are more manageable. But the nights are still reliably difficult. I have been awake at some point on most nights for almost five years. Ben is, apparently, not able to sleep through consistently.

We are used to Ben falling asleep hours after we had first put him in bed then waking up after midnight and staying awake for a few hours. I hear him shouting or snorting on the monitor that I keep next to my bed. I know he won't go back to sleep alone so I put on my dressing gown and my glasses and walk across the landing into his dark room. He is often distressed and needs to be changed then sat up on my lap so he can burp. I then lay him back in his cot and hold his hands, keeping him on his side to allow gravity to assist me in stilling a body that is so awake, so full of unpredictable movement that it seems unlikely he will ever be drowsy. Sometimes I will myself back to sleep in my own bed while James goes into Ben. But mostly I get up with Ben when it is dark and then James takes over with him in the morning, at the first hint of light. I can then sleep for a few hours undisturbed before James appears with a cup of tea, needing to go to work.

When I was pregnant with Max I still found room on my lap for Ben to sit. Often I was so tired I brought Ben into our bed immediately, drawing him into my body and using my legs to weigh him down. I would feel his involuntary movements under my heavy limbs – muscles that twitched but would eventually still when he slept. I knew how far through the night we were by whether I could hear the planes above, heading into Heathrow. Sometimes I would run out of options or patience to get Ben back to sleep and leave him to cry in his bed.

We have tried everything: 'sleep training', medication, positioning systems, diet. Some of it appeared to help before it didn't any more. Occasionally Ben sleeps all night, maybe three or four nights in a row and we feel a glimmer of hope but then he begins waking up once more. No amount of analysis reveals the secret of our success. Sometimes he is awake but content – I'll hear him making his little clicking noises – but mostly when he wakes he is upset and needs us to help him settle. It has been so long since I've had reliable sleep that I think it is normal.

Now that we have received a payment from Ben's legal settlement we have the option of paying for night carers to be with Ben. When it was first suggested to us I couldn't imagine how this would work and instinctively said no. I thought it would feel so invasive to have someone in our house at night and like a dereliction of duty to pay someone to get up with my child. Although I feel resentful that I have to keep getting up in the dark, never getting enough sleep, I also feel maternally possessive and that this is exactly what I should be doing. Mothers get up to their stirring children. 'But don't you think you need a bit more sleep?' James gently asks. It is particularly difficult on my own when he is away with work.

An agency can supply a nurse called Luke who will work overnight and I agree to try it. I meet Luke while Ben is at school and he seems nice, qualified. But what am I looking for in a person who is going to look after my child at night, when all the streetlamps are lit and Ben is expecting one of his parents?

The first night Luke can come is when James is away. This is good timing since these periods of caring for two boys largely on my own are exhausting, but it will mean I have to navigate these new waters alone. I could say no and delay for a week. Instead I agree to show a carer how to comfort my child in the middle of the night while I sleep.

Luke arrives at 10pm on the first night and the night after. I show him what to do. I emerge in my dressing gown to introduce Ben to Luke when he wakes. I try to work out which tasks are essential and which are a mother's or father's work. Ben seems confused but accommodating – I had warned him what would happen. Luke comes for four nights each week for the next few months and he is sensitive to our nervousness. A few months later, we find Beatrice who can come for an additional two nights each week. She has done this kind of work before and is training to be a nurse. She exudes calm capability and from then on we regularly have someone sitting in a room in our house awake all night.

I feel I have lost something in the frequency and familiarity of those quiet dark nights, when I was willing both Ben and myself back to sleep. But what I lose in intimacy and privacy, I gain in clarity: the fog of five years of sleep deprivation lifts and I can see the wood for the trees. With help on some nights and some days I feel less like I'm just coping and more in control. I can spend some time with each child and organize our lives better. There are days when our house feels too small to accommodate all of the people in it and I am frustrated by each person putting Ben's coat in a different place so I can never find it, but I know the kids are better off with more hands able to help them. I still think my hands are the best but they are not always available when they are needed.

A friend who has children of similar ages, an older disabled child and a younger non-disabled child, says she resents needing help. She wants to be able to look after her children on her own and doesn't want another adult, a stranger, around all the time. She doesn't want to be self-conscious about what she is doing, how she is talking, when she loses patience in her own house. I don't feel like that – I see the help we have as a facilitation of the boys being able to do what they should be doing. Ben is able to go to physio groups and be fed when he needs to be, Max is able to go to playgroups and nap in his cot rather than in the car on the way back from an appointment. It hasn't occurred to me to resent it. We are privileged to be able to afford some help and I can see that it is helping us cope. I feel a little less like I'm constantly paddling to keep us above water.

The money from the legal process has also helped put us in the fortunate position where we can now buy a house. House buying is a highly stressful process and this is no exception. Our extensive and non-negotiable list of requirements is based on what Ben and his wheelchair require, and there are very few appropriate houses. Following numerous false starts and a lot of visits to potential properties, I find one that could work and, after months of nervous bureaucracy, it becomes ours. It is a Victorian house on three floors near our rented house and within the borough that is funding Ben's school place. We had briefly discussed moving to a different area with more practical housing stock but we didn't want to move away from all of the things we liked about where we lived, including having family close by. Ben's disability has changed our lives in ways we hadn't anticipated but we don't want it to take us away from the people we love.

The new house is at least twice as big as our previous home. It feels like we have been breathing in, trying to fit ourselves into a house that couldn't quite contain our ever-expanding family with all of its aids and equipment. Now we can exhale. Ben can sit almost anywhere in the house and we still have room to walk around him. Our friend Dan comes back and builds temporary wooden ramps and platforms so we can get Ben out to the conservatory and the garden, even if tall people do have to duck under the door frames. I feel self-conscious about being so privileged, being able to buy such a house and having so much space, but incredibly grateful for it.

We change almost nothing in the house and live our lives with the terracotta walls and sage green tiles of the previous owners' kitchen, in which the fronts fall off the drawers and the fridge freezes all of our vegetables. The conservatory is always too cold or too bright and the door of the cupboard above the washing machine flies off as I open it, cutting my forehead. The study becomes our playroom and we fill the built-in bookshelves with toys and tolerate the blood red walls. The pale blue and pink sitting room reminds me of rooms we had visited in Syria. We move in the table and chairs we bought in Damascus and keep the heavily brocaded curtains up while we make plans to radically redecorate. It feels like a house for grown-ups and we're trying our best to fit in.

Over the next year, we carry Ben up the stairs to his bedroom, a staircase that is conveniently wider than any we have had before but which feels increasingly perilous. We have to buy a stair climber for carers to use – an electric motor attached to a car seat on a frame. Once Ben is in the seat we can lean the stair climber back towards us as we stand on the stairs and at the press of a button the machine lifts him up, one step at a time. It is slow and noisy but avoids carers having to carry him. It is theoretically safer but only if the carer doesn't slip and let go. We know we are running down the clock of how long Ben can get to the first floor of our house without a lift. I know I won't be able to carry him up the stairs for ever.

I am busy with full days and considerable responsibilities but I really want to have another baby. I had always assumed I would have three children (I am one of three siblings), but it has been hard to envisage when James and I are constantly occupied just keeping our household going and everyone in it happy and healthy. We feel like we are almost always about to lose control of something so it would be madness to have another child.

But on the other hand, maybe that's exactly why a third child might be possible – we have become comfortable with a perpetual level of chaos that others would find intolerable. Thanks to our overnight carers I am less chronically tired and it feels like it might be something we can do. James is less convinced but reminds me that I told him I wanted three children when we met 15 years previously and he is eventually won round by the possibility of another baby. In 2015, I become pregnant again.

As with my previous pregnancies, I am exhausted for the first few months but then I am fine and the pregnancy is uncomplicated. I love being pregnant and it makes little difference to how I look after Ben and Max. I continue going to the gym, lifting weights as my bump grows, and I can still carry Ben up the stairs. I feel not just physically strong but almost invincible.

When friends, and particularly acquaintances, find out I'm pregnant they can't disguise their shock. Many of them clearly think we are mad. The pregnancy makes me think about how the dynamics in our family will change and how we will raise Ben and his siblings to relate to each other. Apart from two years of Ben being an only child, everything they have learned about the world has been with each other in the background. They know no different.

All kids look up to those older than them and Max is no different. Ben is almost six, Max is three and he wants to do all of the things his older brother does. He knows Ben is disabled and he tries to work out how people grow and are classified. 'Will I become disabled when I'm older?' he asks, assuming that he will become more like Ben. He doesn't see this as negative, he just asks whether he'll get a wheelchair like Ben's, or go to the same school when he's disabled. There is something bittersweet about Max climbing into Ben's wheelchair when he isn't using it to eat his snack or insisting on wearing Ben's specialist Lycra suit (skintight to improve Ben's posture). I struggle to resolve the difference between Max seeing himself as the same as Ben and strangers seeing them as entirely different children. When we try to take Ben swimming during the quieter disabled swim session at a local pool we are told that Max is not allowed in the pool with Ben because he is not disabled. We should take Ben into the pool between 9 and 10am and Max from 10 to 11am, the lady at the desk says. 'But that's ridiculous,' I say. 'My husband and I both need to swim with Ben and we can't leave Max on his own.' She is unswayed.

Young children are idealists and Max hasn't realized that wheelchairs and aids are not seen as aspirational. I hope it continues like this. I think that Max's relaxed attitude to disability is how we would all be if we came across more disabled people at school and work. I wonder if we can raise another child with the same approach and whether having a non-disabled (I presume, though I know it's not certain) sibling will alter how Max sees Ben. I hope that having a third child is a gesture of optimism – not that we're trying to dilute the amount of disability in our family but that we think our children are brilliant and we would like to have another. I hear other women talk about wanting to have another baby after their disabled child in order to have a chance to do it 'right', to be able to mother in the way they anticipated, but I don't feel like that about this pregnancy. I do hope my pregnancy and birth are straightforward but I'm not having a third baby in order to right a wrong. I feel like Ben's life will only be enhanced by us building his gang, because in our family we're not living in the shadow of Ben's disability, we're open to the light and possibilities.

I do think carefully about what I am bringing this new baby into. There will be disadvantages for Ben as we spread out our time and attention. We already have to interrupt reading a book if his brother needs a wee or is in the midst of a meltdown. Max sometimes feels like Ben gets the lion's share of our attention, of everyone's time. Ben's needs dictate much of what we do – our holidays, the carers in our house, the places we go – and the new baby will have to fit into that.

I also can't protect Max from seeing things I wish he didn't because he is Ben's brother.

One day, Max asks me to teach him how to click with his fingers. When I ask where he has seen clicking, he recounts in painfully accurate detail an incident a few weeks previously when a woman who was to accompany Ben on the school bus was clicking in his face in an apparent attempt to distract or entertain him. When James asked her not to and suggested she speak to Ben rather than click her fingers directly in front of his nose, she got very defensive. 'I am a mother. I know what I am doing,' she said in justification. 'He doesn't like it,' James said to her, 'so you need to stop. You can just talk to him instead of clicking.' We were standing at the side of the road waiting for Ben to board the bus and I was holding Max. The woman continued to argue with us. James and I decided to take Ben off the bus and we returned to our front door while James found the car keys in order to drive Ben to school instead. Max was confused by it all. 'You and Daddy were very cross and the lady was shouting and Ben is in our family,' he said. It is inevitable that this new baby will also witness incidents I'd prefer they didn't.

A chatty three-year-old, however, is a marvellous lubricant in social situations and forces all of us, not least Ben, to look outwards at the world. Max talks to people in shops and on the street. We visit places as a family that we wouldn't if it were just me, James and Ben. And we all laugh more at, and with, Max. We won't produce another baby like Max, because kids have a habit of being their own people right from the word go. But if our third child can be at least a bit as accepting and amusing as Max we'll probably be OK. Having three children is a risk, but I hope it will be worth it.

In the summer before he turns six, Ben moves schools, to one that specializes in assisted communication – communicating without talking, using aids and equipment. This time our dealings with the local authority are straightforward, aided by very helpful headteachers.

Ben has brain surgery over the summer holiday to put in an implant to try to reduce some of his dystonic symptoms (uncontrolled and involuntary muscle movements). It has been long planned and we think very carefully about whether the benefits will outweigh the risks, eventually deciding that if we can give Ben a little more control over his body it is worth trying. Like with Ben's previous surgeries, the process of being in hospital and sending him into theatre is stressful and worrying, and I am pregnant again which exacerbates the amount I cry about it. On the day, I read Knock Knock jokes to Ben in a cubicle while we wait for the surgeons to be ready to take him into theatre. As I work my way through *Harry Hill's Whopping Great Joke Book* my voice breaks and James has to take over. We had planned for me to accompany Ben as he was sedated but I'm crying so much James takes him in. The six-hour wait for the surgery to finish feels interminable, like being in the calm eye of a storm, and when Ben eventually emerges he is upset and in pain and we are buffeted by the storm of his needs and our emotions. For the next four days

Ben is subdued or distressed, with only small glimpses of smiles. His head is wrapped in a bandage and he mainly lies in bed. We gradually build up to him sitting in his chair for short periods, allowing himself to be distracted by TV programmes, a helium balloon sent by friends and books. On the fifth day we are transferred to another hospital and two days later we are allowed to go home.

It is an intense week. James sleeps beside Ben every night and the two of them become so attuned James can tell from a slight flinch of Ben's back, or a particular grimace, whether he is in pain or wants to be held. I arrive each morning, laden with clean clothes, Ben's food and new books, so James can go home to nap. In the 12 hours I'm in Ben's hospital room I can only leave to get food or drinks if one of our family is there to stay with him. There aren't enough nurses to sit with him otherwise, and Ben cries if he's left alone. Max is thrown by Ben disappearing from home and James and me never being in the same place at the same time. Our parents and siblings look after Max, showering him with attention, but he's discombobulated. He is only happy when he visits Ben and sees us together. 'He's like Mr Bump,' he says when he sees Ben's bandage. I find it almost unbearable that both my sons are not themselves. When Ben returns home he is fragile but recuperates with lots of paracetamol and episodes of *Arthur*. Max regains his equilibrium.

Two weeks after surgery, Ben is due to start at the new school. We are fearful of him being at school, especially a brand new one, when he hasn't fully recovered. He is no longer in pain but still has a bandage over the healing wounds on his head.

Despite his physical discomfort and the unfamiliarity of his surroundings, Ben settles in quickly. As we walk in on the first day, Ben is all smiles. He loved his old school and it feels like he knows he will enjoy this one. He's right. I think it's partly because he likes learning and the variety of a school day, and partly because it's an excellent school with perceptive staff. James and I are far more anxious than Ben but the teachers and assistants are so obviously capable that we have no choice but to happily, nervously, leave Ben there and go for a coffee. For the first few weeks, he only goes to school part time and James takes almost a month off work to help steward us through this period, introducing Ben to the new school and people slowly. I am relieved that we have made this transition before the baby is born.

In December, Max and I go to the Christmas play at Ben's new school. It isn't a traditional nativity play – each class performs a segment around a theme. Ben's part is mainly based on the story of the three pigs and the big bad wolf. I become fidgety when I notice the chest strap of his chair isn't quite tight enough. I want to go and adjust it. Ben is, as always, not relaxed. His lips are pursed and his cheeks get redder and redder as the performance goes on, but he takes part without tipping over into sadness. It is a triumph of logistics and imagination.

One of the older classes then performs a piece based on space and they are dressed as astronauts while singing 'All

About That Space' to the tune of a Meghan Trainor song. This happens to be one of Max's favourite songs and he is outraged. 'It's All About That BASS, not SPACE!' he shouts. 'Astronauts are not disabled,' he says loudly. 'Um, yes, well, don't they look great?' I say. 'Astronauts cannot be in wheelchairs,' he says determinedly.

He is a three-year-old who spends a lot of time with disabled children but he is also a typical kid who deals mainly in black and white and is hugely influenced by what he sees around him. In the same way that he's not sure women can be sea adventurers because there are only two female characters on the TV programme *Octonauts*, he thinks astronauts can't be disabled because he has never seen one. And he's sort of right. There haven't been any astronauts who use wheelchairs and it's not clear there will be soon. But it's also pretty unlikely that any of the children we know will grow up to be astronauts despite their aspirations, yet we don't tell them it's impossible. Right now, as children, they can pretend to be whoever they want to be. The whole point of childhood is to have dreams and the role of parents is to make the landscapes of their imaginations as wide as possible.

After Max's comments at the play, I spend a lot of time talking about how he and Ben can pretend to be, perhaps aim to be, astronauts, or whatever they want. The boundary between fantasy and fact is purposely leaky at this stage and is helped by seeing as many diverse stories and role models as possible. Max and Ben need to see disabled people (as well as people from all backgrounds, ethnicities, genders) in their books and on TV, doing the same things that the White, non-disabled, male characters get to do. In order for Ben's mind to be free to roam he needs to not feel excluded before he has started and I need to try to ensure Max sees possibilities rather than exclusions.

I seize the opportunity provided by a massive pile of cardboard from the delivery of a new sofa and, with my scalpel and a roll of packing tape, I make a wheelchair-accessible rocket. My seven years of architectural education have not been wasted. It's big enough for Ben to get into in his chair and still have room for his brother. Max decorates it with neon stars from the pound shop and I cut planets out of metallic card. It has an ill-fitting door to shut out adults and interior lighting courtesy of battery-operated fairy lights. It's crude and not photogenic but the kids love it.

James, Max and Ben between them create an elaborate bedtime routine which involves turning all the lights off and taking a pretend voyage to the moon before Ben is put in bed. Max climbs up into the bed and they play with various light toys and the Buzz Lightyear toy we had bought Ben to reward him for all his hard work at school. For slightly obscure reasons, this is called the Bedtime Disco (though it involves no music). Therapists would call it sensory play.

If the world won't provide the imaginative horizons my kids need, we'll have to create them ourselves. I have high ambitions for them, astronauts or not.

8

On a cold winter's morning at the very end of the year, James and I arrive at the hospital early while the boys are in the care of grandparents. I am due to have an elective caesarean and we are ready for our daughter to be born. I am in compression stockings and a gown as we take selfies in front of the sunrise, complete with the swollen nose that apparently characterizes late pregnancy for me.

We are really hoping our third baby will not need immediate medical attention. It seems to us likely that she will, but numerous doctors have tried to convince us that this baby won't end up in NICU. A neonatal consultant has talked us through the statistics, telling us most newborns don't need medical attention, but Ben and Max did so it's possible. Our obstetrician, who delivered Max and whom we have seen throughout this pregnancy, warned us at our last appointment that she would not be working today as it's the festive period. Once again, a paediatrician will be at the delivery just in case. My excitement at meeting our baby is swirling with apprehension based on experience. I know things can go wrong but I remind myself that lots of people have babies uneventfully. I remain hopeful that we can be one of those people, for once.

We are in a bay within a larger room, surrounded by blue curtains which ensure some privacy but no soundproofing. We can hear other women also preparing for their births. We haven't a clue where we are on the operating list. As I wait on the bed, the curtain swishes as someone enters our bay and I look up.

'Hello, so today's the day! I've just looked at the list and you are second so I'll go and get things ready and we should be able to head into theatre soon.'

'But it's your day off!' I say in surprise as I take in the doctor standing in front of me. Our obstetrician. 'You're not working today.'

'I've just come for you and then I'm back home,' she says as she heads off to change out of her jeans and leather jacket into scrubs. James and I look at each other. 'She's here,' I say quietly to him. We are amazed she has come to deliver this baby, for us. I think maybe everything will be OK.

We walk into theatre as the doctors and nurses are discussing their Christmases and their plans for New Year. 'You know how this works,' our obstetrician says as the anaesthetist ensures my lower body is numb and the operation begins.

Our daughter cries before she is out of my womb, shocked at such a brutal disturbance, and is immediately declared totally and utterly healthy by the neonatologist in the room. No resuscitation, no breathing difficulties, no one at all worried about anything. As she finishes stitching me back together, the obstetrician asks if we would like to go home tomorrow if we can. 'Yes, definitely, yes please,' I say. 'I thought you might,' she says. 'I'll make a note on your file.'

We are wheeled back to the recovery bay where once again Maddy joins us and we tell her our baby is called Molly. When I am taken up to the postnatal ward it is still light outside and James, Maddy and Molly are all with me. We spend the rest of the day and that night on the ward – me in the bed, James now allowed to stay overnight so on an armchair beside me, Molly on the other side in her transparent cot. Molly breastfeeds immediately and when she is finished I tuck her into the front of my nightie and fall asleep semi-reclined on the bed, James keeping an eye on both of us. She sleeps with her cheek squished against my heart, covered with the same stripy blanket that covered her brothers, my hands clasped under her bum. We are in an identical bay to the one I had after Max was born but this time I have a baby with me. I am amazed at how oblivious it's possible to be to the women without their babies, the ones walking slowly out of the ward, past the lifts, and buzzing for entry into the neonatal unit.

I am less aware of my catheter this time because I don't need to leave the ward or manoeuvre myself into a wheelchair. I just stay in the bed. I wake periodically when Molly wakes, I feed her and then we both go back to sleep. Day turns to night, then it is day again but from my bed in the back of the bay I don't register dusk or dawn. I only tell time by the shouts for meals. I am dozy and hazy but I don't begrudge being woken by my daughter or other babies on the ward, or the discomfort of my abdominal wound. I have my baby with me and she is healthy. We don't see any more doctors. The midwives observe her occasionally, no one comes to check her overnight. I am delighted by the relative lack of interest because this is a sign that she is well.

The following day, we leave the hospital with plentiful painkillers, a beautiful baby and everlasting gratitude for the kindness and expertise of our obstetrician. She gave up her day off to make things work for us, to ease our anxieties, and she succeeded. I had only dared to hope, just a little bit, that a birth could be this smooth.

We get home to find Ben and Max have made banners while we have been away. We introduce them to their sister together. When my parents arrive later and ask what the baby is called we tell them to ask Ben. Since he can't talk, he has a communication button which normally goes back and forth to school with pre-recorded messages so he can tell people something about his day, each day's message overwriting the one from the day before. I have just recorded a short message about the baby. James holds the communication button in front of Ben, he bangs his hand on the big red button and we all hear my recorded voice, speaking on Ben's behalf: 'This is my new sister. Her name is Molly.'

We bring Molly into the pink and blue sitting room and James lights a fire as she sleeps in the same wicker Moses basket that her brothers had used. She stays with us all the time – breastfeeding then falling asleep on James. I barely leave the sofa or my bed as we start to negotiate being a family of five.

One week in, when I can just about walk round the block and am craving fresh air, we go on our first family outing, with me slowly pushing Molly in her buggy, James pushing Ben in his wheelchair and Max on his bike. We make it just 100 metres from our front door before Max breaks the rule about how far ahead he is allowed to go alone. We shout, he cries, Ben cries because Max is crying and we all go home grumpy. When we try again a few days later it's less eventful, offering us hope that we might be able to leave the house as a family.

The boys are sweet with Molly and tolerant of the disruption and imposition involved in having a newborn sister. A new day carer, Lydia, had started working with Ben two months before Molly's birth. She immediately built a rapport with Ben that meant he was always pleased to see her and constantly amused by her stories and jokes. Lydia had found new television programmes that both boys watched in rapt attention and initiated craft projects. It had been her idea to make banners to welcome Molly home and she now kept Ben, and Max, occupied while we were distracted by the new baby. With James off work for a month and the help of day and night carers and aunts, uncles and grandparents, we are able to keep things as routine as we can. Ben starts back at school and Max is at nursery part time (the same one Ben went to). It works, but now that we have three children I am more reliant than ever on having help. Molly doesn't like being put down and when I am on my own once James is back at work I have no choice but to sometimes leave her crying in her basket while I change Ben or help Max go to the loo. Sometimes I carry her around the house in a sling and she will doze despite being right next to a loud high-speed blender while I make Ben's food. It's all a constant juggle.

Rather than the dependency of a baby who needs to be fed via a tube, I now have a baby who needs me, and only me, to breastfeed them. Molly refuses all attempts to feed her otherwise and she is with me almost all the time, despite James's best efforts to extract her. She wants to be close and once again I have the soft squish of baby against my skin much of the time, at all hours, and sometimes it is too much.

She wakes a lot at night and though I am relieved at how simple the transaction is – I put her to my breast and she drinks and goes back to sleep – it is relentless having a small baby who wakes repeatedly, sometimes hourly. There is no option but to wake up and comfort her even if I have barely slept. It is so reminiscent of the early months with Ben – the crushing realization that there is no one else to do this, it has to be me. I spend some nights simultaneously filled with love for this squidgy, beautiful baby and crying with exhaustion, desperate to just have a night of uninterrupted sleep. One of our night carers leaves so James goes down to Ben when he wakes while I feed two-month-old Molly in our bed. One night, Max walks into our bedroom wearing a pumpkin suit, so all five of us are awake at 2am, one in fancy dress. We must be mad.

But Molly feeds and sleeps, oblivious, and learns to smile. Other than not liking to be put down in the day, she is otherwise easy to please and, compared with Ben, so simple. We revel in how confident we feel with her, how easy it is to interpret her demands. It feels intoxicatingly joyous that this healthy, thriving baby is ours. She sleeps in our room for far longer than the other two and we are indulgent, knowing she is our last baby and how quickly this first year will pass.

Over the following months, Molly learns to roll and pick things up with her hands. She is my trusty little sidekick when the boys are out. She is totally different to her brothers, but in many ways more like Ben than Max. She likes to be held like Ben did and hates some of the toys and sensations that Max loved as a baby. It makes me re-evaluate which bits of Ben's babyhood were his innate preferences and which bits were influenced by his impairment. I see that so much of what he liked and thought overlaps with his sister and was him, and nothing to do with him being disabled.

We normally have Lydia to help after school, mostly with Ben. She gives him a snack, reads books and bathes him before his dinner. He needs to have a bath before he is fed, otherwise he is more likely to be sick. So I am in the kitchen breastfeeding Molly and sitting with Max as he eats his dinner while Ben is with Lydia in his bedroom or the bathroom, which means we end up dispersed around the house. It's a practical solution to the three of them needing different things at the same time but it doesn't feel quite right having them separated, missing out on the incidental conversation or jokes that come of being in the same place at the same time. Sometimes I shoo Max upstairs once he's finished his dinner to bother his brother, to make sure Ben feels included, while I clear up.

James and I know Ben so well we can generally tell by his movements, facial expressions and noises whether he is happy or not, whether he's in pain or content. Ben has found highly effective ways to compensate for his inability to speak. In some ways, he can communicate well. He can smile or frown, laugh, shout or push out his bottom lip. Looking expectant means 'I'm interested'. Whingeing indicates dissatisfaction. When he is bored of a television programme he makes whingeing noises until we change it. When he has to have a blood test he starts crying as we approach the phlebotomy room and waves his arms in protest. His uncle Harry buys him a box set of Roald Dahl's children books and we work our way through them. When given a choice of four books, Ben can choose which one he wants by looking at it and when offered three picture books and *The Twits*, he chooses the gruesome tale of Mr and Mrs Twit torturing birds, monkeys and each other. He loves language and no longer needs colourful pictures to accompany stories, though he often likes that. But he can't communicate to us what's coming – he can't tell us he feels sick before the inevitable puke. He can't tell us he's hungry to indicate his tummy is ready for some food. We just have to guess, and it's not foolproof.

We have been trying to increase the reliability and precision of his eyegaze pointing. We started with animals and then moved on to numbers and letters. He now uses an eyegaze computer sometimes – he can control the mouse with his eyes rather than his hands and he mostly plays games which help him build skills. We have bought a laptop with a special eye tracker to use at home in addition to the one they have at school. There are games where Ben splats balloons, or races cars. There are some pages with simple language so he can direct games – making the computer say 'more' or 'stop' – and others with phonic sounds so he can spell words. He's made encouraging progress, but it's also inconsistent. Some days he won't spell words he was able to a week previously. Progress is slow. We think Ben has the intellect to express more sophisticated ideas and desires but he needs the tools. So we have been working with his school and with speech and language therapists to maximize his opportunities using augmentative and alternative communication, or AAC, the term used to capture a whole range of communication systems that don't rely solely on speech.

When Ben was five, I did a two-day course on a communication system that I hoped would help him talk to us and everyone else. We introduced a symbol book where Ben could select symbols with his eyes to communicate what he wanted to say. We then installed the same system onto his eyegaze computer. The success of using aids like symbol books is totally dependent on the expertise of the people surrounding Ben to teach him and then interpret his responses. I am trying to learn as much as I can at the same time as him. I am enthused and also nervous, intimidated even.

A typical child hears spoken language for at least 18 months before they start talking. As soon as they are born, people start talking to them and then, a year or two later (over two years for Max), they start talking themselves. So it follows that we should be modelling the use of the symbol book to Ben for at least a year, probably longer, before we expect him to be using it with us. If we were really to mimic normal acquisition of speech, James and I would use it to talk to each other in front of Ben, for years.

Now that we have introduced the book we need to have it available and be using it all the time. When Ben was four, we introduced 'Yes' and 'No' symbols on his chair so he could look at them to answer questions. A while later, the 'No' got puked on so the tape got wet and the symbol fell off. Despite daily good intentions, I didn't get round to sticking it back on for a few weeks and I felt awful about it. Ben's ability to communicate is dependent on others providing the materials he needs. Two years on, Ben sometimes looks at the 'Yes' and 'No' symbols to answer questions, but often won't, and it's unclear whether he really gets the concept of answering a question like this.

Max is still trying to work out how Ben fits into the rules he's learning: he knows 'big boys' walk and babies don't, but Ben is a big boy and doesn't walk. He asks whether Ben can hear him talking because normally people talk back but Ben doesn't. Max already talks to Ben on his terms – he says 'night night' to Ben every night and waits for Ben to look at him because he knows that's Ben's way of saying goodnight back. When Max asks Ben a question he says, 'Ben, can I play with your Peppa Pig toy, YES OR NO!' and waits to see if he'll look at the symbols on the arms of his chair. We are trying to normalize this way of talking within our family.

When Max is almost four, I complain that he talks too much. I catch myself saying it twice, to two different people, in one week. James is away and I am really feeling the intensity of being the primary carer of all three kids but I am shocked at myself. Max is a chatterbox. Some days he will barely stop talking at all. It's a charming mixture of questions, statements and analyses of the varying powers of superheroes. Since Ben hasn't ever talked, I promised myself that I would try not to take Max's speech for granted. There have been numerous occasions when I have been so very grateful for Max's ability to tell us what the matter is when he's ill or what happened at nursery that day. It's only when my patience is thin, and when I have blithely taken my middle son's ability to talk for granted, that I find myself complaining and then later berate myself. There are many times when I am sad that Ben can't tell me what the matter is, or what he has done that day. The red communication button that goes to school with him and comes back with a recorded message from the teacher telling us about his day is a way around this, but it's no substitute for independent communication and it's a clunky way to converse. I want Ben to talk to me – not by speaking, but to use alternative methods to be able to give me a sense of what matters to him, what he thinks, and how I can help.

We are trying our best to give Ben the means to talk. We continue to model his symbol book with him and set up his eyegaze computer regularly. We print out photos of all the things he had done over the holiday so that he can take them to school. I program new pages on his computer so he can use his eyes to describe what he has been doing to his friends and teachers. I am pleased with myself for managing to navigate the software to do this, with only a couple of exasperating moments when I feel like chucking the computer out the window, but I'm even prouder of Ben for using it. Ben loves it – he enjoys showing people photos of Max squashing him in the park and sharing a sloth joke from the *Zootropolis* film we saw at the cinema. But these things are manipulated by us. We choose which photos to include and which anecdotes to tell. Ben can't tell people what he wants to about his holiday. He can only share one of the moments we chose to include. Who knows whether we have included the bits he most enjoyed? When we talk about when we visited an outdoor light show, Max's best, most important, memory is of the chocolates Grandpa gave him, rather than any of the sculptures. Kids experience the world differently to adults and often remember the bits we think are incidental.

We're making little inroads. When Max is climbing a tree, Ben makes a complaining noise and we ask him, 'Do you want to climb the tree?' He looks at the 'Yes' symbol on the arm of his wheelchair and so James takes him out and lifts him up into the branches. Each week at school Ben helps create a sentence and they work on it each day, putting the words in the right order, and sometimes he gets it right.

On one of the first days back at school after a holiday when he is six, the staff in Ben's classroom navigate him to the 'places' page of his communication book. There are lots of symbols on each page. Ben has to identify which symbol of 64 he wants and then communicate it to the person he is talking to using only his eyes. If he gets distracted or confused midway through he can't say that he needs to start again. He has to choose a word to complete the sentence 'I went to the...' and through careful yes/no answers as he works his way through the various symbols with an assistant, she thinks he chooses 'library'. I went to the library. His teacher wonders if he really means library. We hadn't mentioned going there in our various messages to school. But he had gone to the library. The day before! So he had told his class something we hadn't.

Before Max started talking, it was all in his head, he just had to work out how to say it all so we would understand. Ben clearly has so much to say, but no reliable way to say it. This makes me sad – I hate the idea that we are misinterpreting what Ben wants or needs and therefore letting him down. And in many ways it makes me anxious – it is our job (with various professionals) to help him find ways to talk to us and I feel the weight of the responsibility. But mainly I feel hopeful. Ben has started to use the communication systems we are providing and has begun to talk independently. It will take time, but he's making progress.

As Ben gets older we need to start thinking properly about how we will make our house work for him. When I had first looked at our new house I had done so as an architect and I knew we could adapt it to Ben's needs. I liked the street and could see our family enjoying the garden but I also knew the front garden was big enough to accommodate the ramp we would need to replace the three steps up to the front door. I measured the rooms and calculated that we could lose a proportion of the floor area to the lift we would require. The garden was flat enough that a wheelchair wouldn't roll away and the floors laid out in a way that would mean Ben could access almost all of the rooms. The hallway was wide enough for a person to be able to squeeze past a wheelchair. I had been thinking about a house like this for years, one that we could buy and rebuild. I had visited other houses adapted for wheelchair users and watched *DIY SOS* enough to know there were as many ways to adapt properties as there were houses and there was no right way. Each family had their own priorities and budget to work to.

I want our house to work perfectly for Ben and also facilitate the kind of family life we want: lots of people around the table having lunch, kids running in and out of the garden. I want Ben to be able to go everywhere his siblings can but I don't want the adaptations to be the first things people notice about the house. I want it to feel like a typical family home – with living rooms on the ground floor and bedrooms upstairs. Ben should be able to visit us in our bedroom but we also need some privacy from carers in the house. I plan to make us the best house I can and then never move again.

I am aware of what I don't know and what I can't control. I could design a house for the way we care for Ben at that moment but his wheelchairs will get bigger and his body heavier. I can imagine how we might bathe Ben in a few years but not how we will do that when he is 20. I need to design the house to suit a disabled adult in the future and help to envisage how that would work. Some of the equipment he will need will be out of my control, but I will try my best to accommodate it in a way that is as elegant as possible.

As I begin getting advice as to what equipment we will need to build into the house and how rooms should be arranged, we start to realize how these adaptations will help us. We are still lifting Ben into a typical bath but an occupational therapist tells us bluntly that this is dangerous. She is lacking in any of the gentle empathy of therapists we have seen before. As we sit in the sunny bay window of the red playroom, she tells me I can no longer wash Ben in the way we are used to. 'You need to stop bathing him immediately,' she says. 'You can't put him in the bath any more. You will have to wash him in bed.' She presents herself as the voice of truth against my lack of experience and is unmoved by Ben's fondness for baths or by my desire to continue giving him this most basic of experiences. The risks are mainly to our backs rather than to Ben's safety. When I explain that I am willing to take these risks she disagrees. She has come to talk about manual handling and she has found us wanting.

She is probably right. It is potentially perilous for us to be lifting Ben into a bathseat, even if it does lift up to the level of the top of the bath. But other therapists had gently told us we shouldn't be doing something while also showing how we could do it more safely, or talking us through the alternatives. In telling us to stop giving Ben a bath immediately and not acknowledging the emotional implications, she ensures that we ignore as much of what she has said as possible and refuse to see her again. If her job is to help us help Ben while minimizing the risks to us all, she has failed because she can't see that this isn't an impersonal task to which she just needs to apply her dispassionate knowledge. We are parents who aren't ready to give up intimate moments. Yet.

One day a big trailer arrives outside, towed by a van, with a specialist bath inside for us to view – a massive, height-adjustable bath with hydrotherapy jets. This has been arranged by another occupational therapist who is helping us to plan the adaptations work to the house. I can see how much difference equipment like this would make to us all. We have been told that it is easier for carers to shower children like Ben but he hates showers, so I want to get him a bath. With a bath like this it will be possible.

I find an architect who specializes in accessible buildings. I warn her I am also an architect and will be interfering. We work together to finalize the plans for the house and get the necessary permissions. We take advice on how we can lift, wash and move Ben as he gets older. When we have to make decisions I focus on my priorities: maximum access for Ben, maximum ease for all of us. In a choice between sacrificing floor area in the main rooms or the lift not reaching our bedroom, we prioritize the lift. I think hard about floor levels and doorway widths and all of the tiny details that together make a house truly wheelchair friendly. We gradually realize the scale of what we need to do – the house will be almost demolished before it is rebuilt. I hope we are doing the right thing. Perhaps these old houses aren't for a family like mine.

We find builders and a temporary house to rent nearby just in time for when they are ready to start work. With Molly just over six months old, we pack everything up – again. On the day we move, I sit on the floor of the echoey, empty sitting room breastfeeding Molly while James finishes packing up the last of our belongings. The sofas have gone and there's no fire burning, but the cornices and tall sash windows that we love so much remain. I hope that the disruption we are about to embark upon will be worth it.

9

When Max starts at a local primary school they ask us to send in photos of his family. A few weeks later we see the pictures they have been making in class – a large flower where each petal is covered in one of the photos from home. Next to one of him and Ben lying together a teacher has written Max's description: 'Me and Ben are lying in bed. Ben's disabled and my bed isn't that big so he sleeps downstairs.' Other petals talk about a trip to Legoland and when I painted his and Ben's faces on holiday in France. On the back, Max has written his and Ben's names and drawn pictures of them both – big round bodies with stick limbs and prominent belly buttons. They are both standing and Ben is bigger than Max. Both smiling.

I am nervous about Max starting school because it is the first time he's been somewhere without us where no one knows Ben. I wonder how he will explain Ben to other kids and adults and worry that someone will say something insensitive and make him self-conscious. Actually, within the first two weeks he's watched videos of Paralympians, cheering on Jonnie Peacock, and it's clear that Max is more than happy explaining Ben's disability himself. At Christmas, Max makes only one card at school and chooses to give it to Ben.

There is much discussion about beds though. Max is preoccupied with where he and Ben are sleeping and his favourite game is one where he lies in Ben's bed, hidden under the duvet, and James or I put Ben on top of him. 'Oh Ben, your bed is feeling a bit lumpy!' we say as Ben giggles and wriggles his body around in excitement. From beneath the duvet we hear laughter and eventually Max pushes Ben to one side, shouting, 'I'm squashed!' Molly likes to do this too and we plonk her in Ben's bed, on top of him. She squirms around, pushing her arm into his face which he is surprisingly relaxed about. She is so comfortable with the particulars of Ben's body – she can now pull herself up on his wheelchair and braves his unpredictable arms to be close to him. She grabs his hand when she can and squishes her cheek into his when we let her. He finds her amusing, even when we make a big show of making her apologize to him for peeling off the 'Yes' and 'No' flashcards we keep Velcroed to the back of his chair and putting them down the loo, and when she pulls his books off his shelves and chews the corners.

These squashing games almost always happen in Ben's bed because his bedroom is on the ground floor of our temporary house and it's becoming difficult to carry him to Max's bed upstairs. Max nags us to be allowed to sleep a whole night in Ben's room. 'Why can't I have a sleepover?' he asks. Eventually we relent and put an inflatable bed on the floor at the foot of Ben's bed. James carries Ben over to Max's bed for once and they lie next to each other laughing at their dad's jokes while Ben's legs kick continuously in excitement. We return Ben to his own bed and we say goodnight to them both, turning off the fairy lights and tucking them under their duvets. They both look too pleased to drop off but they do. The sleepover is a success.

Building work gets going at our house and I feel like it is being destroyed. I visit often, parking Molly's buggy in what had been the sitting room but is now the site office, where the carpet has been ripped out and the sofas replaced with plastic chairs but the brocade curtains remain, gathering dust. I carry Molly on my hip as I walk around with the builders. Each time I am there another hole has been made or something else ripped out. The work is tearing apart walls that have stood for a hundred years and cornices that I treasured. It feels unseemly to be exposing the innards to public view and to be causing this much disruption for a dream.

At the temporary house, Ben still needs to be carried upstairs to have a bath. The problem now isn't so much the lifting, though that is less than ideal, but the baby. Molly is crawling and then toddling and is not safe around stairs. When I am on my own with three children I have to plan carefully how to bathe them without Molly falling downstairs or me tripping over her while carrying Ben. I need someone there to help me and if I'm the only adult I hate having to choose between one child's cleanliness and another's safety. I resent that the doomsday therapist was right as I start washing Ben in his bed. When James and I get Ben into the bath together, Molly joins us in the bathroom, pulls herself up to standing and throws each individual item of Ben's clothing into the bath with him. She chuckles, which makes Ben laugh. Max hears all the noise and comes running, falling over with hysterics when he realizes what Molly has done while I fish out soggy socks.

Molly learns to walk just after she turns one and we all coo. It looks so unlikely as she waddles around like a little drunk person, walking a few more steps each day. It seems near miraculous that she has learned to walk on her own with so little help from us, even though I know this is what Max did. She improves rapidly and is obviously pleased with herself, even when she drops to her bum often. Whenever anyone asks how Molly is we tell them proudly that she is walking.

I start to wonder how Ben feels about Molly learning to walk on her own. Is he sad that she is doing something he can't? When we congratulate Molly, does he hear an implicit criticism of him not walking? They are quite obviously very different children but I feel like we're sending a strong message that walking is triumphant. I rein myself in and spend a day or two trying not to talk too much about Molly's walking, acting as if it is no big deal.

One day, Max, then four, asks me if I am better at maths than him and I decide to tell him yes, I am. I have an A level in maths. I don't go on about it, but I tell the truth because we can't spend the rest of our lives not being honest about who is good at what and what one of us can do that the other can't do as well. Some of our kids will be good at remembering obscure cricketers (James's genes), some will be good at chemistry or craft (my genes). It's pretty unlikely one of them will be talented at everything so they will all have to experience that irritating feeling of knowing your sibling is better than you at something. In Ben's case, the nature of his disability is such that he will do lots of amazing things but some physical skills will constantly elude him. Max and Molly will do things that he can't.

The danger isn't in being truthful about what one child can do and risking implicit criticism of another. The danger is in exalting some skills above others – in having a hierarchy of achievements and comparing them against each other. Walking is useful but not essential. 'Isn't it a shame that Ben can't walk along walls like Max can?' a parent says to me as we are walking together. 'No, I don't think it is,' I reply and ask them not to say that in front of our kids. We can praise Max's balance without comparing him with his brother. All comparisons do is taint an otherwise pleasant walk.

Avoiding direct comparison is tricky with Max's constant questions comparing me with James, James with Superman, Superman with Spiderman, etc., but we try. Ben won't walk unaided, but his school annual review lists 'walking' (in a supportive frame where he is strapped in and his weight supported, with his feet free to touch the floor) under the list of 'What Ben Likes'. Ben started using a walking frame when he was two and we bought one for him to practise in at home.

It is difficult for him to co-ordinate his movements and tiring over even short distances, but he enjoys it. Now the walking frame is at school and he can roam the corridors, very slowly and effortfully. Each child is on their own track. I just need to enjoy watching Molly negotiate going downstairs backwards and Max learning to write. These gross and fine motor skills are easy for parents to take for granted. I do not. I see them for the incredible feats of co-ordination that they are.

I belatedly realize I haven't asked Ben what he thinks about Molly's walking. I sit down with him and his eyegaze computer and use his communication software to say what I think by selecting the words I want. 'Molly – walk – great', I make the computer say. I then ask Ben what he thinks of Molly's walking. He chooses a phrase on his device by looking at the screen: 'I don't want to do it', the computer says. He then selects another word: 'Good', before refusing to engage with the discussion any further and getting frustrated that I am delaying him listening to *The Faraway Tree*. I take from this that he doesn't want to walk like Molly but thinks it's good and I suspect I have overthought the whole episode.

As Max starts his second term at school, Lydia leaves. It's a surprise and leaves us with less help during the day – after school and during the school holidays. It's not that we don't have any help – we still have overnight carers who get up with Ben when he wakes and spend hours preparing his food for the following day. I'm still woken in the night by Molly, but their help is very useful nonetheless and the stability of our night carers is what keeps our day-to-day lives on track. Beatrice, one of the night carers who has now been working with Ben for almost two years, is supremely capable, no-nonsense with us and solicitous to Ben. Another night carer, Rose, started six months previously and is gentle, entertaining and reliable. I am so grateful for the consistency of these women, regularly arriving at 10pm ready to take care of Ben so we can get some sleep, leaving pristine rows of syringes of food in the fridge ready to go the next morning.

Lucy had started working with us in the autumn on Saturday mornings and for a few hours on Sunday. It has taken some time for us to work each other out and for us to adjust to having someone in the house at the weekend but she soaks up the feedback we give her. By the time Lydia leaves, Lucy is another dependable member of the team keeping Ben cared for and entertained. It means James and I have some hope of talking to each other at the weekend, perhaps taking one child out alone. She comes with ideas for craft projects and brings her own books that she thinks Ben will like, which he does because her instincts for Ben's interests are spot on. Lucy now helps after school when she can, but most days I am alone with the kids. We keep trying to find a new carer but for multiple reasons we can't: we find someone who only works for one day before never returning; we offer another person the role but they don't accept because they are worried that if Ben dies they will be unemployed. We interview several people who have no experience looking after a child like Ben and don't seem like a fit for our family.

Molly is at home with me during the day while Max and Ben are at school and James is at work. She accompanies me to showrooms and builders' merchants as I choose fittings for the building works at our house and then we collect Max from school together before walking home in time to meet Ben off the school bus. I wrangle the three of them until James gets back for bedtime. Sometimes my mum or Prudence can help, or Maddy (now with her own small baby, Ralph) but mostly it's just me.

Max makes friends at school and I make friends with their parents. He starts having friends over to play and, as these kids and their parents visit, Ben meets an ever-widening circle of people. I get to know these families well enough to ask favours of them occasionally and it's a revelation. Ben has never had local friends in this way, and the ease of getting to know other parents by walking to school with them and then being able to ask them to pick up Max one afternoon is wonderful.

Two families live very close to us and they include Ben in the Christmas presents they drop off. They are friendly to him and sensitive to how our family is different. Max can't do any afterschool activities unless our new school friends can deliver and collect him, which they happily do. Max doesn't know that he isn't having swimming lessons like his friends or that they are going to the park after school. He has no sense of missing out and I'm relieved. I don't want him to resent his siblings and the complexity they add with either their disability or their age. When I do have help one afternoon,

I take Max (and Molly) to a local adventure playground with his friends, and the combination of the play structures and being somewhere new after school blows his mind. 'This is amazing, Mummy!' he shouts at me before running off.

We have five months of only occasional weekday help and I try to simplify our lives in this period, cutting down the risks of something going wrong or of spreading myself too thin. I can't pick Ben up from school because I need to be simultaneously at Max's school, so Ben gets the bus home every day. Molly has to fit in with what I am doing but is increasingly mobile and uncontrollable. She can slip away from me and does, more than either of the boys, so I try to be at home as much as possible. I feel like the three children are the vertices of a triangle pulling me in entirely different directions and it's difficult to make it work. Even the most basic parenting – feeding and changing them, keeping them safe, washing them occasionally – can be overwhelming when the days are repetitive and relentless.

They watch a lot of TV. Molly marauds around putting things where they will trip us up or get squashed under Ben's wheelchair and I find myself raising my voice. I just try to make it through until James returns from work – a fresh face with apparently plentiful energy and patience. When he travels with work I strip my ambitions back to absolute basics, knowing that the work he does is worthwhile but also wanting him to return as soon as possible.

One afternoon, I strap Ben into his standing frame, and find time to sit next to him with Max on my lap while

Molly rearranges Ben's bookshelves. I read a chapter of *Harry Potter and the Philosopher's Stone*, which we gave to Ben for his seventh birthday. Balancing the book between my knee and my right hand, I put my other hand on Max who pushes it away because he says he is too old to be held. As I read a sentence, Max tells us 'four' and 'more' rhyme and Ben smiles at him while wiggling from side to side. Introducing books like this to them is fun.

By the time World Book Day comes around, we have finished *The Philosopher's Stone* and Ben has also watched the film. I dress him as Harry Potter – drawing on slightly wonky glasses with black facepaint so they have some chance of lasting the day. Ben would shake off real glasses within minutes. I make an owl out of card, drawing on the feathers, and I attach it to the frame of the wheelchair so Hedwig perches just above Ben's shoulder. As we go out to the school bus we stop just in front of a full-length mirror so Ben can see himself as Harry and he smiles, almost immediately dropping the wand that I had made out of rolled paper and tried to wedge in his hand. When he returns that afternoon, the wand has disappeared but the costume is otherwise intact and when I ask if everyone liked him being Harry Potter he looks to answer 'yes'. I am so pleased for him.

There is otherwise little light in the wintry afternoons and evenings of the early part of 2017 and no imminent hope of respite. I love my children and we have delightful moments but there is so little time to read books and laugh at jokes or do any of the things with them that I like. I am too busy getting food ready and changing a nappy to initiate a game. I don't do the physio with Ben that I should. They all have different needs, physical and emotional, at one, four and seven years old, and I'm so bogged down in the monotony of meeting the most basic of needs that it squeezes the joy out. I am at capacity with entertaining Ben (who cannot be left bored), preparing his meals and medication, feeding Max and Molly, cleaning up, getting bags ready for school, shopping, ordering and washing. I wish that I could look after the three of them on my own more competently. I want to be happier. I chose to stay at home and mother my children but I begin to feel like I don't have a choice. I'm stuck in the toil of daily feeding and wiping.

When I do take them to the park on my own (Molly in a sling, me pushing Ben in his wheelchair, making Max hold onto the wheelchair when we cross roads), I am extremely pleased with myself. When James is away on a Saturday I take them all out early, knowing that the park will be quiet and we can then be in the house for the rest of the day without feeling guilty. Meanwhile, far from resenting their relative confinement, the kids are getting on with each other brilliantly. Having practically ignored Max when he was a baby and toddler, Ben is now amused by Molly climbing up his chair and onto him when he is lying on the floor. He tolerates her, and their cousin Ralph (only six months younger than Molly), shouting right next to his head. Max can now make Ben laugh and uses Ben's eyegaze computer to crack jokes for us all. We invent a game where I ask the boys a question, like 'Am I ever irritating?' Ben looks at his computer which has three symbols: 'Yes', 'No' and 'I don't know'. When he looks at the symbol he wants, the computer says 'Yes'. It is a touchscreen computer as well as an eyegaze device so Max then selects the answer he wants – 'Yes' – and I pretend to be outraged while Ben and Max laugh hysterically. 'I am never irritating!' I shriek. Max throws back his head in laughter and Ben looks to Max as he's giggling. When Max stands next to Ben's wheelchair, holding onto the armrest for support, they are the same height, have almost identical hair and look so similar as they share the same joke.

In these moments I am not thinking about Ben's impairments, but day to day the unadapted temporary house combined with being on my own a lot exacerbates how disabled Ben feels to me. I am more aware of his disability when it is difficult to handle his body or the equipment he needs. When I have to think a lot about whether I can get him to a bath safely or if I can carry him out to the garden (which is down a long flight of steps), I am very aware of what his body cannot do and what I need to help him with. The same is true out of the house – we are most aware of how unusual his body is when we are the exception or we have to make a fuss because buildings don't work for him. In small spaces, his wheelchair feels huge and in quiet rooms we are hyperaware of the noises he makes.

We used to be able to make access work for Ben by sheer force of enthusiasm and physical strength, by lifting him and his chair to where they needed to be. Sometimes one of us would carry Ben and another carry the chair. Other times, between James and myself, we could bump Ben and his wheelchair up a couple of steps. As he has got bigger we have needed more people: faced with a whole flight of stairs we need three strong adults. We do this for Christmas dinners on lower ground floors and afternoons with friends in first-floor flats. As Ben and his wheelchairs get larger it is becoming less feasible. When we are invited to people's houses we start to ask how we will get to their front door and whether there are any steps inside. We are less likely to take Ben somewhere we haven't been before in case there's some issue we haven't anticipated. And at home I can no longer take him into the garden spontaneously – I have to plan carefully and wait until there are other adults around. Ben's level of disability isn't a fixed point that I can get used to. It slips and slides according to how onerous it feels to push his chair around or carry him to where he needs to be.

His impairments have not changed over the years, he has just got bigger, and because the physical environment has not changed to match his evolving needs, he is less able to do what he wants or needs to. This is what it is to be disabled.

One weekend, James and I drive to a park where we know there is an accessible roundabout. We pull open the stiff gates to wheel Ben onto the roundabout and lift Molly onto one of the seats, telling her to hold on tight. Max climbs through to the middle and holds onto a rail as we begin to push. The roundabout is old and heavy, even without the weight of Ben and his wheelchair, so it takes two of us to get up some speed.

As the kids' faces rotate past us we can see that all three are happy. 'We want to go as fast as a rocket!' Max shouts. It's hard work keeping the roundabout going and a man in the park with his daughter comes to help – until Molly starts to climb off her seat and we have to stop. This roundabout is the only thing in a playground that Ben, Max and Molly can do together and all enjoy. I love seeing them on it, three thrilled faces rushing by, but it makes me wish that I could bring them here more often and I can't on my own. I want more afternoons when Ben's disability is irrelevant to him being able to do something he enjoys.

A community nurse first told us about the possibility of respite care when Ben was five. She referred us to a hospice and they offered us 12 nights a year when Ben could stay with them, without us. I was ambivalent about being offered 'respite'. Respite from what – from looking after my own child? It felt defeatist to admit that we needed a break and that we wanted Ben to stay somewhere strange without us. Since Ben was a few months old he had regularly spent days and nights with his grandparents but any child of mine, disabled or not, would have done that. He was familiar with their houses and we were lucky to have capable, close family able to do this but as he got larger it had got harder. We decided we would try the hospice.

After numerous conversations, the hospice said Ben could only stay if he was fed formula milk. Letters from his doctors saying he was healthiest when he ate blended food were ignored. Our dietician said she was unable to intervene and the hospice said they did not have the right protocols in place. By this point he wasn't being fed any milk at home and when he had last been fed formula regularly he had vomited frequently. I couldn't let him stay in a strange, new place, being fed milk that might make him sick, so we declined the offer of respite.

Eighteen months later, when Ben was six, we found an alternative hospice and, with Molly in tow, we visited without Ben and spent two hours going through every aspect of his diet, medication, likes and dislikes. This hospice would be able to feed Ben the food he was used to. It was a formal nurse-led healthcare setting with the protocols, gloves and charts of a hospital plus art and sensory rooms, workshops and trips. Everyone was friendly but our meeting was in a quiet room with butterfly artwork on the wall and I just knew this was the room where parents spent time after their child had died. In some ways I wanted nothing to do with this place. I didn't want to classify Ben as a burden from which I needed respite. But I also knew it would be good for Max to have his parents' attention for a weekend. We could visit places that Ben didn't like or couldn't access, while he was being read books, watching DVDs and playing with therapists. We decided to give it a go.

On Ben's first visit, James and Max stayed in a flat upstairs so James could help the staff get to know Ben and be on hand for any questions. Max was thrilled – the hospice had plenty of toys and a little garden, and he loved the idea of sharing a double bed with his dad. Ben was OK with unfamiliar people feeding and entertaining him. James appreciated Max being there, to take the edge off an otherwise intense situation. I slept at home in a strangely quiet house with baby Molly, who was still breastfeeding during the night, and I was relieved that this let me off the hook.

I found it overwhelming when I went to the hospice during the day. I was reminded of hospital stays when the nurses called me 'mum' rather than my name. The reality of teaching the nurses how to look after Ben made me want to either take him home immediately and hold him close or leave him there and pretend, or hope, that he was OK. I wanted to delegate responsibility for his care for a day but I also didn't want to trust strangers to look after my precious child. I was conflicted and kept bursting into tears that weekend but Ben wasn't upset and the staff were able to do everything he needed. It had been a success and he was set to return a few months later to stay on his own for a night.

The weekend Ben is due to visit the hospice again, it takes a few hours to pack up everything he needs. When James and Ben leave, I call ahead and it transpires that the staff don't think Ben is arriving until later in the day. I had just about steeled myself for Ben staying away, alone, and the notion that they are not expecting him sends me over the edge.

I ring James in tears and he swears in frustration. 'I'll sort it out,' he says, 'don't worry.' He returns a few hours later alone, saying everything is fine and Ben was happy when he left. We spend the afternoon with Max and Molly, taking them to a playground that Ben doesn't enjoy and then returning to a quieter-than-usual house. I spend most of the day anxious that I'm not making the most of the time while also worrying whether Ben is OK. I had anticipated it being really relaxed, but we still have two children and Max bursts into tears three times over the weekend because Ben isn't there and he wants to be at the hospice too.

That night we go out for dinner to celebrate our eleventh wedding anniversary, appreciating the ease of organizing babysitting for two non-disabled kids. We eat and drink too much, fade far too early and come home to Molly screaming in the babysitter's face. When James calls the hospice – I don't like calling because it makes me feel awful that I am having to ask someone else how my own son is – they say Ben is asleep.

We wake up to a house that only has two kids in it and us, which is unusual – no night carer. We potter around in dressing gowns with only Weetabix for the kids to think about. We go out for lunch where we are just about able to have conversations with other adults at a table with benches that wouldn't accommodate a wheelchair. I have fun but feel distracted, slightly ashamed that Ben isn't there – even though we probably wouldn't have gone for the lunch at all if Ben had been here because of the difficulty of access, the noise and the chaos of three children.

James calls the hospice from the restaurant and they tell him Ben is happy and well. When Ben comes home he is thrilled to see me, Max and Molly. He smiles at us as James wheels him into the kitchen and I am relieved that he looks relaxed. He doesn't have the tense body and pursed lips that

I had feared after an anxious time away. Max is so happy to have Ben back that he is even content to forgo his favourite television programmes in favour of something Ben prefers. They sit next to each other at the end of the kitchen table watching an iPad as usual and equilibrium has been restored. We get into a rhythm of Ben staying at the hospice for a weekend every six to eight weeks. When the weeks are fraught and exhausting, in the absence of a carer to help in the day, the hospice days and night become a welcome period of relative calm and reduced intensity.

One day, Ben's carer Lucy meets us at the hospice as we drop him off. James and I talk to the staff and unpack Ben's medications as Lucy sits and reads to Ben. She stays for a few hours after we have left to make sure the staff understand what Ben wants and needs. I now feel confident that the nurses can feed and physically care for Ben but I am still worried they don't know what books or films he likes and how he communicates his opinions. Having Lucy there for a bit makes me feel better as she can help the nurses to learn Ben's preferences. When she leaves she texts us: 'Just leaving. Ben was settled but a bit upset when I left, crying.' I reply to ask if he was crying because she was leaving and she says yes. James phones the hospice and they say Ben has recovered. I think about him all that weekend, wondering how often he is sad that we left him there, though when we collect him he is happy.

Ben carries on going to the hospice every few months. One weekend he comes back with a joke book that he has made with one of the nurses, a smiley Australian who listened carefully when we said Ben liked jokes. I am so thrilled to have my guilt overwritten by evidence, in book form, of the fun he has been having and he smiles broadly when we read the book to Max. I am glad we accepted the offer of respite.

10

'Cheers!' I say to James as we clink our plastic cups together and take a sip of the champagne we have brought with us. We are standing on the new terrace of our house, looking out over an abandoned broken fridge to a garden which has been destroyed by building machinery. Max and Molly have been given strict instructions to stay away from the digger in the garden and are pottering around the empty house, while Ben sits next to us listening to an audiobook. Behind us the house is wrapped like a present – billowing bags over light fittings and plastic sheets over brand-new carpet. It is mid-spring of 2017 and our house has been rebuilt. We are just visiting, revelling in the ease with which we can wheel Ben up to the front door and through it. Piling into the new lift, we wonder if the novelty will ever wear off.

Over the previous nine months, the house has been pulled apart and painstakingly put back together especially for us. Some doorways have been widened and new doors fitted.

Others have been blocked up and new openings created by hacking holes in Victorian lath and plaster. Wiring and pipes have been removed in huge quantities and then carefully relaid before the walls were patched back together. We watched the opening up of the shaft for the lift with amazement – a monumental metal-lined hole three storeys high. We made decisions about sockets we would later regret and agonized over minimizing thresholds between rooms, making compromises about floor finishes in order to avoid even small steps up or down. I have marked out mountains to be painted on Molly's bedroom walls and the decorator has used a laser to paint a circus big top on Ben's ceiling, refusing my offer to simplify the design because he relished the challenge. Brick by brick, new ramps have been built at the front and back of the house. Huge new sliding doors promise unfettered access to the garden. It feels like the house we lived in before but also a totally different place, with novel views through new doors and an unfamiliar ease when we move around it with Ben. He has visited the building works once before – our builders solicitously putting down temporary boards so his wheelchair could get in, and beaming when we told them how much Ben had loved the lift.

As soon as Ben and Max return to school after the Easter holidays in mid-April, we move back in. The days are lighter, and although I am still finding things very intense, at least the house is now ready. It is the sixth house move we have done since Ben was born seven years ago and we are relieved it will be the last for a while, if not for ever.

From the temporary house that was too dark, multi-levelled and strange we move back to our own house which is now fresh and welcoming. It feels like getting a new bespoke pair of glasses after years of smudges and discomfort. We start to inhabit the architecture, choosing a dining table with a shallow top so Ben's knees can fit underneath in his wheelchair but large enough to seat lots of friends around it. We put shelving all along one wall of the dining room to display the kids' artwork and pile up the books that Ben likes, away from Molly's inquisitive hands. There are also bookshelves in Ben's room, the sitting room and the playroom. Ben likes a book called *The Bookshop Girl* and we joke that our new house will be like the home of the character in the story who lives in a second-hand bookshop with piles of books everywhere.

Years earlier, someone had said to me that the house was the thing that could make the biggest difference to the everyday happiness of a family like ours. They weren't downplaying the importance of having help from carers, or good health, but assuming those aspects weren't onerous, the house could make or break your day. Now that we are living in a house that works for us, I can see even more clearly how previous houses had worked against us.

I'm still often on my own with the kids which restricts what we can do, but when we come home from school, Max, Molly and I sit on the sofa reading while looking out the front window for Ben's school bus. When the bus arrives, I go out to meet him and wheel him back in, up the ramp and through to the back of the house, with no bumps or jolts. I give Ben his snack while he watches TV and the other two play or join him as I cook their dinner. I read them all a book while Max and Molly eat, stopping so we can all hear the message from school recorded on Ben's communication button. As Ben slowly pushes the red button, we hear his teacher telling us Ben did PE today and recounting his favourite activity.

When the other two have finished their pudding we all go upstairs in the lift, squeezing around Ben's wheelchair and Max helping me to press the button. Molly and Max get out toys in the playroom while I give Ben a bath next door, doors open so they can shout to me. When Ben is out of the bath they get in while I dress Ben in pyjamas and start to give him his dinner. Molly still has tantrums and Ben still gets annoyed when he can't hear over Max's shouting, but I feel more capable. The house helps me look after all three of my children simultaneously as it accommodates us, rather than walls and steps being in my way. I have some control over my days, which makes me a better mother. I don't have to choose between them as much. It shouldn't be a luxury to feel able to bathe your child whenever you want to, but it feels like that, and I am grateful for it.

By May, we see that the wisteria in our garden has survived the building work as it begins to flower. We put a hammock outside and James lifts Ben into it with me. Max climbs in too before Molly also waddles over and demands to be lifted in. She crawls all over us and Max shouts at her but Ben doesn't mind. It's chaos with four of us squashed in there. When it rains we all get out and open up the doors to the dining room, bringing the stripy hammock inside so Ben can sway on his own. We play him Justin Timberlake and he wiggles and bucks to the music, making noises that mean he loves it. The hammock fabric falls closed above his head so I can't see him, just the outline of his wobbling suspended body like a chrysalis about to hatch.

One of our night carers leaves and we recruit another, Sofia, who is capable, quiet and a welcome presence in the house. The turnover of carers can feel near constant, even though some stay for years. As we head towards the summer, we interview candidates to help in the day and meet someone we really like called Mel. One of her references is from the mother of a disabled child that she had worked with previously and I read that the reason Mel left that job was because the child died. The reference is generous and positive with an extra hand-written page setting out all the ways in which Mel is professional and 'delightful'. That this mother has written this reference, less than two years after her child passed away, seems like the highest possible recommendation. Mel starts working with Ben just as the summer holidays start, so she is plunged in the deep end, spending 11 hours a day with us.

Mel is the 18th carer we have employed to help us look after Ben, yet I am still struggling with the language to use. 'Carer' sounds old-fashioned to me with connotations of older people needing support, of deterioration and medical supplies. For a while we used the word 'nanny' but it sounded a bit Mary Poppins and didn't encompass all of the ways in which

Ben was helped. Disabled adults often refer to their 'personal assistant' or PA, which I like, but what kind of child has a PA? So for the moment we stick with the word carer.

We have been looking for a carer to help with the basic aspects of Ben's life: to get him where he needs to be, meet his basic requirements for food, water and toileting. A typical child becomes more independent as they grow but Ben will not. Mel has to confidently connect the feeding tube into Ben's tummy and feed him and feel comfortable moving him from his wheelchair to his bed. She learns how to wash him and change his clothes quickly and without fuss. We ask people to undertake these most personal of tasks with Ben – those of dependency, vulnerability and utmost practicality – and it always feels like a risk when we employ someone new. It is necessary that Ben relies on other people to help him with his day-to-day life but he gets very little say in who helps him or how, and we don't know if Ben will like new people.

For good carers, these crucial but everyday tasks come naturally: Ben is cared for and this leaves room for more interesting pursuits. In the past, we have had carers who were trained actors and read books to Ben as if they were on the stage and he was their audience. Mel brings enthusiasm, dedication and humour – within days she has clocked which books Ben likes and which jokes make him chuckle. She uses Ben's communication book to tell him about something she saw in the street that she knows he will find amusing. Max wants to be with Ben and Mel and she chats away to them both while effortlessly working her way through Ben's daily routine. Soon all three children will be crowded around whatever game she has started, even though they have only known her for a month. Mel is a brilliant example of what happens when we have the best people around us: I can do all the bits of mothering that I want. I can read books to individual kids, give cuddles, cook meals, while Mel does physio exercises with Ben and prepares his medication. I'm able to take Max to the park after school and then look at his homework while Ben is bathed, or Mel can pick Max up from school while I take Ben to an appointment. Mel not only looks after Ben, suggesting museum trips and making sure his eyegaze computer is working, but also communicates with the rest of the carer team. It's better than doing it all myself and I appreciate the help.

With the privilege of having regular help throughout the week and at night, I wonder how we balance having carers with delegating too much of our parenting. What we gain in sanity, we lose in mundane intimacy. With Mel there regularly I can go weeks without giving Ben a bath myself. When Max asks to share a bedroom with Ben it means both boys are woken early by a night carer – Beatrice, Rose or Sofia. I have gained sleep but perhaps I have sleepwalked into losing some everyday moments, the relentless accrual of small tasks which make up parenting. In the absence of any role models for this kind of mothering, my gut instinct tells me it's weird that someone watches my child sleep, however kindly, and possibly knows more than I do about how Ben fidgets during the night, while I sleep.

Towards the end of the summer holiday, James and I leave Max and Molly with Mel at home and take Ben to the Natural History Museum. Having Mel around is as much about us being able to spend the day with Ben as it is her helping with him. There is a butterfly house and we push Ben's wheelchair through two layers of plastic curtains into the hot humid building. As we start walking along the path, a man in a butterfly-branded T-shirt walks past, saying hello, and within moments he has returned with a huge dead butterfly for Ben to look at. It is bigger than his outstretched hand with pristine yellow and green wings and brown eye-like patterns. He brings it close to Ben so he can see it clearly and I hold Ben's hands to stop him accidentally swiping the creature, which looks like it might take off at any moment, onto the floor. We thank the butterfly keeper and continue around the path, manoeuvring Ben's wheelchair past groups of visitors and trying to get him close to butterflies feeding on slices of ripe fruit.

As we go past the hut where new butterflies hatch, a different keeper sees us and comes out holding a tray covered in chrysalises of every type – light green and dark brown, small and large, some patterned, others smooth and consistent. She holds one up in front of Ben's face and it looks like a nugget of gold – shiny and hard. Ben looks carefully and then looks away in the hope that we will move on but I ask lots of questions, remembering what metamorphosis involves and amazed that a pupa can be so beautiful. As we then head towards the exit, the male keeper finds us again, this time holding a cut orange upon which a large brown patterned butterfly is feeding. He brings it down to Ben's eyeline and other visitors crowd round to look. Ben gazes at the butterfly and then up at the keeper as he explains which type it is. When people go out of their way to show Ben things he cannot get close to, I am touched. We thank the keeper effusively while escaping to the fresh, dry air of South Kensington.

We walk over to a new building at the nearby Victoria and Albert Museum and James runs around the courtyard pushing Ben, skidding on the smooth stone and both of them yelping as James narrowly avoids crashing. The kindness of the butterfly keeper may be the highlight of my day, but this bit is undoubtedly Ben's.

Ever since Ben and Max watched the film *Sing* we have been listening to the soundtrack. Halfway through lifting Ben between the changing plinth and his wheelchair one afternoon I pause. I am now using a hoist to lift him so Ben is suspended in a fabric sling from mechanical machinery attached to the ceiling of his bedroom. I can lift the sling up and down with a handheld controller and I raise him just high enough to be clear of the plinth and pull him away from the bed and the walls. As Elton John sings 'I'm Still Standing' I spin Ben round. Now that he's too big for me to sway him in my arms, this is a way of giving him the sensation of swinging. He likes it, his body calm and still within the centrifugal force of the rotations. Max and Molly ask to have a go and once I have lowered Ben into his wheelchair I strap each of them into a sling and spin them like Ben. 'Again!' they shout. 'I'm still standing,' they sing.

The hoists are a safe, if slow, way of moving Ben now he is heavy. Our carers and Ben's school have been using them with him for the last year or two. When Ben is in a sling – a shaped piece of specialist fabric with straps and loops – we can attach the sling to a hoist bar and then lift him up and down at will. Our carers had been using mobile or temporary hoists but now they are integrated into the house.

Although we never articulate it to each other, I think James and I feel like the hoists are for other people, the ones who are paid to take care of Ben. Whereas we really love him so we will lift him with one arm cradled under his neck and the other under his legs like we always have. The act of using the hoist has become entangled for me with an idea of Ben's disability being unmanageable as he gets older. Hoisting feels formal, slow and distant whereas lifting him feels natural and right. James always lifts Ben. I want to keep lifting him but some of the joints at the base of my spine do not and I have already had a period of acute back pain. I know that carrying and cuddling will be slowly replaced by the attachment of a sling to a hook, the pressing of buttons and the whirr of a machine as my habits are forced to change by the ache of my vertebrae. When I use the hoist I tell myself it isn't a defeat.

Ben is, and has always been, relaxed about being hoisted. This is an issue for me not him. I hold onto the smooth curve of his body within the sling while he, almost inevitably, fidgets and kicks because that's what his body does. I want to keep the physical connection, for us to both remember the joy of him being on my lap and me cradling him in my arms but it's getting harder to do. I resent equipment mediating my relationship with him but it's also hard to be a good parent if my back hurts, so I try to incorporate spins with Elton John or moments of swinging. Over time, I get better and faster at using the hoist and it feels less annoying. It gradually becomes normal for us and, eventually, as Ben continues to get heavier, the only time I don't use the hoists is when he is sick in his bed and I carry him over to his changing table in a hurry.

There is an inevitable layer of formality that comes with hoisting. We need to check that everyone knows how to do it safely. We arrange for Ben's carers to have manual handling training from a specialist who comes to the house since the implications of him growing are not only emotional and physical but bluntly legal. I have joined these training sessions before and it's strange being given a certificate of attendance for remaining in my own home. The language is about mitigating risks and identifying dangers and it feels odd that there are meetings and assessments about the perils of caring for my son's body. James and I stay out of the way for this training, leaving Mel in charge. I know that she will protect Ben from having to hear his body described as a risk. Ben is happily watching TV as it starts and I talk to the visiting trainer about the need to keep him out of earshot for as long as possible. I don't want him to hear them talking about moving him being difficult because I worry that he will come to feel that he is the problem. I have bought an adult-sized sling so they can practise on each other before needing to see Ben being hoisted into his wheelchair.

After the session, the trainer has a query about the hoists and says she will call the company who installed them. 'There is no need,' I say and respond to her question. I know this house and all of the equipment in it intimately. I can answer almost every query and if I can't then I have the mobile number of someone who can. I have specifically designed the house to minimize discussions about how difficult Ben's body is to handle. I may not be an expert in hoists but I am in my house and I will do all I can to seamlessly manage Ben's body as it grows.

Now Ben is heavy we have no choice but to engage with aids and adaptations for his needs and the accompanying professionals and risk-assessment processes that come with them. We can't ignore the physical implications of Ben's disability but we can attempt to handle them as gracefully as possible. We have made a house in which Ben is least disabled: his impairments are unremarkable at home where he can go upstairs at the push of a button, easily be moved from wheelchair to bed and visit every room. I realize what a radical political act it seems to be to believe that Ben isn't the issue, the world around him is. In our house, his disability is not a problem and I won't let people tell him it is.

Ben's need for carers means our house is not private – James and my bedroom and bathroom are the only rooms that are truly our own, the rest is a place of work for the carers and specialists we employ. The personal nature of what carers need to do for Ben means his room is not just a boy's bedroom

– with hoists, pads and gloves there is a danger it becomes a medical bay as well as a training venue. I try to push back against this – to find places to store the more medical materials so that they are not immediately visible. I make posters of his favourite word: 'Supercalifragilisticexpialidocious!' and mount them to the wall. We display the Buzz Lightyear that Ben loved when he was five and the Harry Potter Lego that he got for Christmas. There are books everywhere and a mirror ball with a spotlight which, on dark nights, makes the room look like a magical cave. This is Ben's room not a hospital ward or a hospice room.

Ben's room is purposely at the centre of the house. It's on the middle of three floors which means we all go past it, or through it, multiple times a day. When Ben is with a carer I will spot them through the door and say hello, putting away a pack of medical gloves that has been left out. Our bedroom is above Ben's room and when he and Max sleep they have wave sounds playing in the background, white noise to encourage undisturbed nights, which we can hear from our room. We can also hear the sound of the hoists sliding along the ceiling below us like rolls of thunder and the reverberations of the lift descending. Even if I am not in the room, I can hear what Ben is doing. Sometimes I would like to be oblivious to all of the goings-on, to turn over and sleep rather than be reminded that someone else is caring for my son. But mostly it means I know what Ben is up to even if I'm not the one doing it and in this way I remain intimately connected to Ben's days and nights.

The house works for all of us. I feel lucky to be able to live here, proud to have created our home and guilty that I have such a house. I assuage my guilt by hosting parties and inviting people over, trying to share the house with as many people as we can manage. When we were doing the building work a friend, who also has a disabled daughter and was adapting her house, joked that once our houses were finished we would be able to visit each other, if no one else. She was sort of right – it's now rare that Ben goes to a party at someone else's house, but we have a big summer party at ours.

The house and garden fill up with friends and their children and, even with three children in wheelchairs, there's space for everyone to mill around. When it is too loud, Ben goes out into the garden, later returning to dance in the kitchen. When Max spins him, he accidentally scrapes the cupboard with the wheelchair footrest and I don't mind. Maddy's partner, George, has set up decks and as I hold Molly and James twirls Ben in his chair, he plays one of my favourite Caribou tracks: 'Can't Do Without You'. It's all exactly how I hoped it would be.

When Halloween comes round, Max campaigns to be allowed to trick or treat for the first time. He has heard about it at school and since it apparently involves sweets he is keen. We arrange to go trick or treating with a few of his friends and their mothers, my friends. Both Ben and Max are going to dress up as Harry Potter and I recycle Ben's Harry Potter costume from earlier in the year but make a matching Hedwig owl for Max which we attach to the shoulder of his bin bag cloak. I draw scars on both of their foreheads, and wonky glasses once again. Mel has made a broomstick with Ben this time, entirely unprompted by me, so we strap this to the front of his wheelchair. It has sticks made of floppy card and Nimbus 2000 written on the handle. I put fairy lights on the back of Ben's chair and around Max's loot bucket. Molly is too young for this adventure so she stays at home with Mel and it's just getting dark as I walk around the corner with the boys to meet our friends and start finding houses with lit pumpkins outside.

I bump Ben up garden paths and across gravel to get to front doors. Our friends go slowly so we can keep up and call their kids back when they sprint ahead of Ben. He is often hidden behind a gaggle of kids shouting, 'Trick or treat!' and if the person answering the door doesn't spot him, Max says, 'I'm going to take an extra sweet for my brother,' pointing over his shoulder. Some people come down their front steps to give a treat to Ben and I thank them while putting it into my pocket. Ben can't eat any of these sweets but we can give him a little taste. As we come to the end of the route, we line all the kids up on the pavement and take a photo of them, our friend's daughter squeezed up against Ben's chair. The kids are high on sugar and thrilled with their bounty. I had been dreading the evening, envisaging teenagers in scary masks, Ben being bored and houses with lots of steps up to their front doors. I had only agreed because I didn't want Max to miss out, but it has been unexpectedly fun. The friends we make through Max's primary school absorb us, making us feel like we're part of a local community in a way we hadn't had before, and it makes us feel like we belong.

When Molly is two she starts at the local nursery. Many of the staff that looked after Ben and Max are still there and the building is practically unchanged. It feels nostalgic to settle our third child into the nursery. They talk to Molly about her brothers, telling her what they were like before she was born. Some time after she has started she tells me, in toddler speak, that there's a boy at nursery with a chair like Ben. When I arrive to collect her one afternoon I find her riding a trike around the garden while her friend sits under a tree with staff in an identical chair to Ben's. He has similar movements to Ben and the way he is sat with nursery workers is so reminiscent. My daughter's keyworker tells me that when this boy started at the nursery some children were nervous about his chair and how to approach him. 'Molly went and said hello and held his hand,' he says and tears come to my eyes. 'My friend is like Ben,' Molly tells me later.

A few months later, Ben and I walk round to the nursery to pick Molly up. She is thrilled to see us both. 'Benny, Benny, Benny,' she shouts as she climbs up onto his wheelchair and squishes her face into his. As we walk home she holds one of my hands while I push Ben with the other. This is a relatively long distance for her to walk and for short periods she climbs onto the side of the wheelchair. She manages to jam her feet on the frame just above the brake and cling onto Ben's armrest like a small, human sidecar. It looks exhausting and I'm not surprised that it doesn't last long. On the uphill I have to negotiate for her to walk on her own so I can use both of my hands to push the wheelchair up the incline and over the bumpy tree roots. Ben is quiet and happy for the journey, which is not always the case.

Molly asks who is at home, and I say there is no one there. She is confused. 'Where is Mel?' she asks. I say that Mel is away. 'Where is Lucy?' she asks. I remind her that Lucy has moved to Scotland. 'Emma?' she asks. 'No, Emma was there this morning but she is sleeping now,' I say.

Molly runs through all of the other carers she can think of. She has much better speech than Max did at this age and although it's not always clear, I admire it. It means she can ask about a long list of people. Emma is a new night carer since Rose, who has been working overnight with us for over a year, has now changed to a mixture of days and nights. Some of the carers Molly asks about are people she has known since she was born. I explain again that there won't be any carers there when we get back. It will just be me, her, Ben and later Max and Daddy. She is convinced I am mistaken. She is so used to there being people in our house she finds it confusing when there are none, and she does not like to be confused. 'Beatrice will be there, Mummy,' she says. She won't, but I don't have the heart to contradict her again.

When we get back, we go up to Ben's room and I start getting him ready for a bath. Molly is playing in the room next door and suddenly comes running in and shouts nonsensical sentences at us: 'There's a bunny in the playroom!' she shrieks which makes Ben laugh. When Max arrives home with

James a little later, Ben is clean and in pyjamas and we all go downstairs while I make dinner. Ben listens to an audiobook by his current favourite author, Kaye Umansky, while everyone is talking around him. Molly is tired and collapses on the floor in tears at a terrible injustice involving an illicit permanent pen. Then she finds a couple of chocolate coins that Ben had brought home from school the day before. She stands in front of Ben, holding the coins up, and asks, 'Can I eat this chocolate, Ben? Yes or No?'

'Mum, he said yes!' she shouts across the room to me as she starts eating the coins without having looked to see Ben's reply to her question. Ben is smiling. There is exactly the volume you would expect of two noisy children, a quieter child listening to a loud story about Prince Dandypants and two adults attempting to discuss their days. The level of noise is almost too much and I keep telling various people to be quiet, but it's also exactly what I hoped for and expected from my family.

That night, Ben won't settle at bedtime. James and I are eating dinner with the video monitor in front of us and we can see Ben waving his arms around, bucking his body and complaining. Sometimes he drops off to sleep after a while but not tonight. After an hour or so, James says, 'I think I'd better go up.' Often when this happens, we have done something wrong (left the light on, not put the white noise on) or Ben needs to be repositioned before he can get to sleep and his noises are his way of telling us this. Luckily Max remains asleep next to Ben despite all the noise. When James comes back down having resettled Ben, and we can see on the video monitor that he is now going to sleep, he says, 'He was really, really pleased to see me.'

It is bittersweet. Disturbed evenings like these are the exception rather than the norm now. It is always lovely for your child to be pleased to see you, but one of the reasons Ben is so happy is because he isn't used to his parents coming in to see him at night. He is used to a night carer and he doesn't realize that the night carers don't arrive until 10pm.

So much of mothering is mundane – years of wiping, feeding and entertaining – but some of it is magical, and occasionally it is both at the same time. I know my children in detail, which is a gift, but also have the broad responsibility to try to make their lives good. I hope that the memories of me having time to listen to their stories, to bake biscuits with them and read *Harry Potter* last longer than those of me not being the person they first saw when they woke. I wish I knew whether we are doing the right thing, if we are choosing the right carers, if we are correct to bring these people into our home. I hope they remember the fun they had with Mel and Lucy and the early morning solicitous care of Beatrice and Rose. I hope they realize when they are older that I wanted to do it all, be it all, in the daylight and the dark, but I couldn't.

11

'You've got your hands full!' the lady said. I smiled in agreement as I released Molly from the carrier on my chest. She had just turned one and was grumbling because she hadn't yet had her morning bottle of milk. I parked Ben's wheelchair next to me in the reception area of the health centre and he began scrutinizing a TV showing footage from four security cameras as I rummaged in my bag to find Molly's bottle without her falling off my lap.

The lady was in her seventies, smartly dressed with immaculate make-up. She was sitting in a wheelchair nearby and, as Molly guzzled the milk I gave her, I turned to the woman. 'She loves milk!' I said.

We had a brief chat about how old the kids were, how cute Molly was and how I had another child at school that day. 'Is he able to go to school?' she asked, as she glanced at Ben. 'Of course,' I said. 'He goes to a brilliant school which he loves, don't you, Ben? We're just here today for a wheelchair appointment.'

I could see a telltale tilt of her head as she looked at Ben. 'He loves school. He goes every day. He likes learning and gets to swim and has great friends…' I said quickly, trying to pre-empt the pity that I knew was coming.

'It's so hard for these handicapped children,' she said. 'So hard for their families. I feel so sorry for them.'

'Oh no. Don't feel sorry for us,' I said as a taxi driver arrived and pushed her out of the building. Our conversation had been cut short and I wasn't sure whether I was relieved or not.

I had no idea why she used a wheelchair, or how old she was when she first used it. I didn't want to minimize Ben's challenges but he was having a good life, most of the time. (And really, which child is having a good life all of the time?) He had fun, he laughed most days. He had a brother and sister who adored him. He had been on holidays to Cornwall and France that year. I wanted to tell her she didn't need to feel sorry for him, or me. I hated that she felt it was OK to talk like that in front of Ben but relieved I got to briefly refute her pity before she disappeared. A few moments later, Ben was called into his appointment and I was distracted by conversations about adjustments and a potential new wheelchair.

Now that Ben is eight, I am so used to his wheelchair, and his need for it, that I think I am entirely accepting of it until I am presented with a new chair and I find myself upset. It seems enormous and I see only how much harder it will be to take out, to squeeze in and move through the world. It will be more difficult to carry upstairs and we might not be able to shove it onto trains without a ramp. I resent the imposition of it into our day-to-day life. I don't like the magnitude of it or the crude metal bars or the weird furry fabric. But I also know Ben needs a bigger chair and so I accept it with conditions – if the base is black and the fabric is different. When the new chair arrives, Ben sits very patiently as a technician fits it around him, while listening to *Harry Potter and the Philosopher's Stone* on audiobook. The technician ranks each Harry Potter book in order of preference as she works.

I don't notice Ben's wheelchair most days, like I don't notice my kids growing. When we see something every day we forget to actually look. Sometimes when I am reunited with my children after a few days away from them it's like I'm seeing them anew. I register the proportion and feel of them with a jolt – simultaneously familiar and surprising. It is like that with Ben in the new chair – it is him in a wheelchair, which I know so well, but he looks taller, older and more relaxed. It makes me feel I must have been squeezing him into a ridiculously small chair before, like I had forgotten that he was eight years old. I see the wheelchair anew and note the engineering and size of it.

There is a hint of melancholy – part of me wants to preserve my child in aspic, prevent the need for larger equipment. Each new chair is that bit bigger, a little bit clunkier, and I have a moment of adjustment. New chairs shout at me with their unfamiliarity and I have to re-accept that this is what Ben needs. I remind myself that this is an aid rather than a punishment. I remember that it's the boy that I love, and he needs this chair, and that soon I will be grateful for it again.

Happily, though, pushing the new chair is a dream compared with the old one – no weird knobbly bits on the handle, much less veering unpredictably into gutters. It comes with a tray which is useful. There is just enough room on the side bar for Molly to hitch a lift, though don't tell wheelchair services that. I sign a disclaimer saying we won't hang or attach anything extraneous to the chair – not bags nor small girls – but we all know I will.

Ben is perfectly happy in his wheelchair and it opens up possibilities, like ice skating. Ice is one of the few environments where people in wheelchairs experience no inconvenience, while walking people are near-incapacitated by the slipperiness of the surface. Only experienced skaters can step out onto an ice rink and confidently glide immediately – most of us need to cling on to the side for a bit, or to gratefully hold Ben's wheelchair, appreciating its solidity. It is a joyful surprise that Ben can be wheeled straight onto ice with no adaptations and little friction.

We develop a tradition of ice skating frequently in the winter. We discover that Ben likes to go as fast as possible and pretend to crash into people or barriers. Somerset House becomes one of our favourite places to skate and we book a slot each year, first thing in the morning, which means leaving home shortly after breakfast. It's midwinter so only just getting light when we cross the river and turn into the grand entrance of Somerset House, having booked one of the best disabled parking spots in London in the grand, classical courtyard. We unload ourselves and all of our cold-weather gear and head to the rink. When Ben is nine, one of the guides comes up to us and says he recognizes Ben from last year. 'Hello,' he says to Ben. 'Let me know if you'd like me to push him round,' he says to us. We ask Ben and he confirms he would, and a short while later the guide takes the handle of Ben's chair and off they go.

The guide is a very accomplished skater so he accelerates quickly and deftly propels Ben through the crowds of tentative skaters. When he finds space he spins Ben round before continuing their anti-clockwise laps of the rink. We are taking a risk – earlier that winter a guide had done something similar at a different rink and Ben had been so sad when it finished that he cried – but we can't deny him this moment. It's balletic to watch a skater with a wheelchair like this – all swooping curves and lightness of touch – and when we catch sight of Ben's face it is lit up, radiating joy. Just as we think this moment has come to an end, a second guide steps in and Ben gets another shot at zooming around before the session finishes. As we are all herded off the ice, and those of us wearing ice skates start removing them, the guide keeps Ben out there and for five minutes they have the ice to themselves surrounded by twinkling Christmas lights.

I read a blog by a disabled woman, Tonia Christie, about her experience of growing up in America. She describes looking back at photographs of herself as a child where her family had wanted her to 'look her best'. 'I listened to the way my family spoke about me and my adaptive equipment (which is very much a part of me),' she writes. 'My walker makes me worse, so I stand far away from it.' She therefore has few photographs from her childhood with her walker, crutches or wheelchair. Tonia addresses her writing to parents of disabled children: 'We may not understand all your words and their implications in that moment but we remember how it made us feel.'

We have plenty of photos of Ben in his wheelchair (or home chair, or standing frame, or walker). But we also have photos where we have taken him out of his wheelchair so that the chair isn't in the photo, so he 'looks his best'. I have taken photos of his face (not his body) because I think this is most photogenic, but also because I don't want the knobs and handles of a wheelchair in the background. We had professional family photos taken and none of them included Ben's wheelchair.

We presume competence with Ben. We assume he can understand everything we say and I try to avoid people talking in front of him negatively. But I hadn't really thought about the impact of talking about his equipment, or of the cumulative effect of a lifetime of us trying to move the wheelchair out of the photo, or trying to crop the equipment out of the frame. Some of this is tied up with the specifics of this particular equipment – the aesthetics of a wheelchair that I didn't choose. Some of it is my natural tendency to try and style some photos of the kids and simplify the background. But Ben already sees few children like him on TV or in books and now I realize we risk editing his own history to minimize the presence of his chair – the very thing that allows him to fully access the world. His wheelchair isn't a sign of weakness.

When I hear other parents discuss their child's first wheelchair, one saying 'you can't polish a turd' in reference to the chair, I see the struggle that I felt at the time and feel ashamed that I had some of those same feelings. I hope Ben doesn't realize that I resented his wheelchair so much. I hope he never conflates how I felt about the chair with how I feel about him. We can criticize the specifics of the equipment (a footplate that won't stay at the right height, an irritating strap) and teach him to have high standards of what he is given but I resolve not to let him hear us denigrate something so intrinsic to his life.

Ben isn't doing as much physiotherapy as when he was younger because I am no longer trying to fix his impairments but rather avoid his muscles tightening and becoming painful. Physio helps build strength and stability in his torso which means, among other things, his head control improves and he can more easily control his eyegaze computer. The aim is to help him to do what he wants to do within the parameters of his body: to play, communicate, sit. He is doing private physio at home once a week as well as a physio session at school, which is less than some children we know and more than others. I don't know what the 'right' amount is. The years of physio have not led to dramatic improvements but he is slowly, slowly getting stronger and he doesn't seem to be in any discomfort.

The tone of Ben's body, and the amount he can control it, varies depending on his mood, fatigue and emotion. His body shifts constantly. When I come into his room one Wednesday afternoon he is sitting on his big green rubber mat on the floor with his physio, Sarah, and she mouths to me that he's been sitting unsupported for over three and a half minutes. He has his legs crossed and is leaning forward a little on straight arms.

Molly is sitting next to him, also cross-legged, and they are watching a programme on the iPad propped in front of them. Ben is uncharacteristically still and by the time he overcorrects a wobble and Sarah catches him he has been sitting on his own for seven minutes which is a record. I am amazed. It is unusual for him to move so little. To see him sit like this, a nine-year-old sitting next to his smaller sister, he looks like a different child to the one I think I know. It's taken years of physio and his hard work to get here. Sarah helps Ben lie down on the mat and I move the iPad to the side so he can still see it. Molly moves too and sits so close to Ben's head that her hip touches his scalp and Ben's now-waving arm threatens to knock over the bowl of melon she has in her hands.

'Why don't you move over here so Ben won't spill your fruit?' I ask her.

'But I want to be close,' she says and strokes his cheek before carrying on eating.

'He did so well!' I whisper to Sarah. 'I know,' she says as we grin at each other.

Molly helps me as I am putting Ben's foot splints – rigid plastic braces to keep his ankles and feet straight – on one morning by picking them up off the floor each time Ben kicks them off.

Ben's growing body is long so as he lies on the plinth in his bedroom, with his limbs in constant motion, objects regularly get kicked or pushed off. 'Why is Ben kicking me in the face?' Molly asks as she climbs back up with the splint. We have talked about this before but I remind her that that her brain is in her head and it tells her legs how to move. 'Ben is disabled and the messages between his brain and legs get confused so his legs kick when he doesn't want them to,' I say. She listens and then starts singing us a song about days of the week.

I think that much of people's discomfort with disability, and their inability to talk about or to disabled people in a way that isn't rude, patronizing or dismissive, is because they don't have the language. Many adults have little experience of talking to disabled people and are not comfortable with which words they are meant to use. If adults don't use straightforward language to talk about disability with kids, and rather refuse to discuss it or use opaque, unfamiliar words, it reinforces the idea that there is something to be scared of or intimidated by. Which is the way most people have grown up. When this happens children think there is something awkward that parents don't want to discuss and they associate that discomfort with people rather than with language. But kids are never too young to be given the words to describe different kinds of people. We have these kinds of conversations with Molly all the time and when someone asks her about Ben she says: 'My brudder is bisabled!'

The rich variety of humans means people like to be called different things, but I use disabled as a descriptive term not a slur and it is the most appropriate word to describe Ben along with 'boy', 'White' and 'male'. Disabled is a political term used to describe people who are disadvantaged and excluded by others because of their impairments. That definitely applies to Ben. When I first meet people and tell them I have a disabled son they often apologize or pity me, like the woman in the health centre waiting room. 'Don't be sorry,' I say. 'He's great.'

Other people with impairments like to use other words. I have friends with children with learning difficulties who describe their children as having special needs rather than disabled. Some adults don't like to be described as having 'special needs' since they would say their needs aren't special, they are specific. Everyone should get to choose how they want to be described.

It can be hard to know what the right thing to do is. I have read accounts by disabled people talking about how horrible it is to be stared at and other articles saying parents should never tell a child to look away from a disabled person because it compounds a sense that there is something taboo about disability. I know that having a child who points and stares at someone, possibly saying something deeply uncomfortable very loudly, is awkward. It can be embarrassing. I also know that having a child who is stared and pointed at can be painful, but most children are just interested or inquisitive. They wonder why Ben is different and the majority of their questions are simple: 'Why does he need a wheelchair? Why doesn't he eat food?' These aren't offensive questions; they are attempts to understand. Parents are often embarrassed because they realize they don't know what to say and are unprepared for this discussion, but often listen carefully when I answer because their child has asked a question that they were too self-conscious to ask themselves. Perhaps they realize how little they have taught their children about disability.

Years before Molly was born, Ben had come with me to take Max to nursery. Ben had left the nursery the year before, so many of the kids, and most of the staff, still knew him. As I negotiated doors that didn't stay open, pushing a wheelchair with one hand and holding onto Max with the other, a whisper went around the room that Ben was there. A little gang of two-, three- and four-year-olds came over and crowded around Ben, touching his legs and holding his hands, which he didn't enjoy. A three-year-old girl pointed at Ben's mouth. 'That's disgusting,' she said. 'No, it's not,' I said quickly. 'It's just dribble. He's dribbling because he can't help it. Ben's not disgusting.'

Ben's lack of control of his tongue and mouth means he can't talk or eat but he also can't control his saliva. He can't stop dribbling, and if he is excited, nauseous or stressed (such as when six children are crowding around him) his tongue whirrs around in his mouth increasing the amount he dribbles. I dabbed his mouth with the bandana he always wore (which we called a bib when he was younger) and was distracted by Max's keyworker coming to take him out of my arms.

The girl didn't intend to be mean. She wasn't old enough to realize any of the implications of what she had said. If we took everything small children said as insults then the locksmith who had come to our house the day before might have left when Max told him he was a bum. My instinctive reaction at the nursery was to take offence on Ben's behalf but three-year-olds mainly repeat what they have been told, and so it was important to explain why Ben was, and is, not disgusting.

In the past, we had put patches of medication behind Ben's ears to dry up secretions and reduce the amount he dribbled, but after nights spent holding him next to the steam from a hot shower in order to clear congestion, we decided it wasn't worth it. We were used to his dribbling. The bandana had become his signature look and some days he could wear the same bandana all day and we barely noticed an issue. Other days we got through more bandanas and dabbed his mouth frequently. Ben occasionally got a sore chin which we slathered with cream but otherwise I wasn't convinced he realized he dribbled or particularly minded. There were options to surgically reposition salivary glands, or take or increase medication, or inject Botox. All of these would involve recovery periods, side effects, disruption. We decided we wouldn't intervene, but had he noticed the girl saying he was disgusting? I didn't know whether we should reduce his dribbling to make him more acceptable to strangers, in order to avoid him hearing insults.

My aim is for our children to grow up thinking they are enough. I want Ben to have a sense of who he is that isn't formed out of the projections of other peoples' fears and ignorance. I don't want him to feel like he takes up more space than he is worth, or to force him to be a certain way because it's perceived as more palatable.

I have explained to many children that Ben is disabled – that his body works differently and he cannot always control it. I have answered Max's friends' questions about why I am connecting a tube to Ben's stomach and pushing water through a syringe, or why Ben is dribbling and how his eyegaze computer works. I am happy to explain all of these things because none of it is problematic for me or Ben. A lot of it is technologically amazing. Most children just want straightforward answers to their questions so they can file it away in the appropriate category in their heads and then they will be less likely to use words like 'disgusting' and be more comfortable with people with impairments.

Molly has a friend come to play and they pick up some teddies. One of them has a button in its tummy like Ben. 'This teddy is bisabled,' Molly says as she shows her friend, 'and this one is a monkey.'

I read an essay by the writer Rebecca Solnit, 'The Pigeonholes When the Doves Have Flown', about how we use language to organize the world. In doing so, we necessarily use one word to encompass huge variation: the colour blue, the concept of love, people as Black. The categories are useful as description and self-definition but can also be the basis for discrimination. Each category is porous and subjective, useful or not. It is good to view people as individuals but in some ways their experience and opportunities will have been determined by their categorization. Nuance in thought and words recognizes the exceptions, the leaks between the categories and the overlaps. 'If language is categories – rain, dreams, jails – then speech is about learning how to conduct the orchestra of words into something precise and maybe even beautiful. Or at least to describe your world well and address others fairly.'

I appreciate the power of defining Ben as disabled – a word reclaimed by those who own it. It is a way to identify a community within a society that can feel hostile, a linguistic way of articulating discrimination and finding belonging when people may otherwise feel isolated. I see it as a way to ally ourselves to others, a useful word to communicate that Ben has access needs, that he is different to other kids. But the variation within a cohort of disabled people is as wide as within humankind. There are children with cerebral palsy whose bodies behave very differently from Ben's and children with entirely dissimilar impairments that Ben has much more in common with. Categorization can be imprecise. I realize the boundary between non-disabled and disabled is hazier than I had thought. When do we flip from one to the other? When does the exclusion begin? Everyone is on sliding scales of skills, impairments and needs which shift and often defy categorization.

Some people aren't interested in any of the nuance of this. They are happy to lump people into groups with reckless abandon – sometimes provocatively, sometimes thoughtlessly. As I become more carefully attuned to the language I use, I notice the words other people say, like using 'retard' in conversation – not only on radio and in podcasts, but our friends. They are trying to describe someone, perhaps themselves, as stupid or clumsy and don't know or don't care that the word has been used to dismiss people with mental or physical disability for generations. 'She is such a retard,' friends say casually as they talk about a politician within earshot of Ben. Because they are our friends, who I know to be good people, I don't always pull them up on it, which I later feel ashamed about. I presume that when challenged they will be apologetic and say they don't think of Ben as retarded. I will believe them. They will ignore the history of individuals similar to Ben being categorized as 'retarded'. Being insulted. They will not see that they are using words which tell us that being disabled is interchangeable with being laughable or inferior.

As Ben and I both get older, I become bolder. When a friend describes a politician as a 'fat spastic' on social media I send him a message. I don't go into detail about spastic being a medical word to describe the tense muscles often associated with cerebral palsy. I don't say that many of Ben's friends have bodies which are spastic. I don't say that I am ashamed to remember calling people 'spastic' in the school playground when I was young, always as an insult. I say, 'I don't like "spastic" as an insult.' 'Agreed,' he writes back. 'It is thoughtless and unpleasant. I'm sorry.'

Language is important, particularly when describing people who often have less power. The words we use matter and we should take responsibility for how we talk about, categorize or insult people. I will watch what language my children hear and teach them how to respond to it. I cannot avoid Ben, and his siblings, hearing language that I would rather they didn't – words that are designed to belittle and abuse disabled people. I will do my best to minimize it, but it is going to happen.

Sometimes the individual words aren't the problem; the assumptions people make about disabled people are betrayed by the way they talk to me or Ben. Or the way they don't. Ben gets ill when James is away travelling for work. I feel like after nine years of being his mother I should be better at managing Ben's illnesses, especially routine viruses that every child gets. But with each cold or cough I feel anxious and this is only made worse by James being away. I feel all of the responsibility and impending sleep-deprivation of having to make decisions alone. When Max and Molly are ill they can now mostly tell me which bit hurts, or if they are thirsty, or if they are not hungry. Ben cannot and I have to guess how much water I can give him. If I give too little he will be dehydrated and unable to tell me he is thirsty, too much and he will be sick.

By the third day of this particular virus I am worried that Ben is listless and has been vomiting a lot. I don't know whether his drowsiness is general malaise due to illness or if he is seriously dehydrated but I can't get even a flicker of a smile out of him and I am concerned. It's late afternoon and I call an out-of-hours GP so I don't have to take Ben to hospital. A couple of hours later, a doctor arrives at our door.

'Is this a children's home?' the doctor asks as she comes through our front door. 'No, it's just our house,' I say as I follow her up the stairs. As we walk into Ben's room, he is in bed and she doesn't say anything to him. She starts to unpack

her equipment and asks if I have alcohol wipes, which I don't.
'I try to make sure my equipment is really clean for children
like this, but if you don't have any then I can't clean them. I'll
just wash my hands.'

I show her the sink and, once her hands are clean, she
checks Ben's temperature, oxygen saturation and heart rate,
leaning over him in his bed so her long hair falls into his face.
'Is he always this passive?' she asks. 'No,' I say. 'That's why I
called you. I'm worried he is dehydrated because he's hardly
kept any fluid down for two days.'

'He's not dehydrated,' she says and packs her things away.
'Just give him regular fluids and paracetamol. Take him to A&E
if you are worried, or call us again.'

As she leaves she doesn't say goodbye to Ben. I feel like I
wasted her time even though I went with my gut and I am
relieved that he has been checked. She spent ten minutes in
Ben's room assessing his health and didn't speak directly to
him once. Ben moans in the bed and I too feel like crying.
'It's OK, Benben,' I say as I stroke his hair. 'She's gone now.'
My mum is in the room next door with Max and Molly and
overheard the conversation. 'That was odd,' she says to me.

I imagine all doctors would say they treat each patient as an
individual but this doctor assumed Ben couldn't understand
what she said and didn't think he deserved a greeting.
I presume that's because she thinks children 'like this' are too
disabled for her to bother. She lumped him into a category
because even medical professionals, who should know better,
are capable of sweeping generalizations and casual rudeness.

I know that interactions with doctors needn't be like this. A year earlier, Ben had again been ill when James was away (there was frequently an unfortunate correlation between the two). He had been coughing and had a fever. After a phone call with my brother-in-law, Harry, and my dad, both doctors, I decided I needed to get him checked. Maddy, George and Ralph came over to be with Max and Molly while I took Ben to A&E with my mum. We saw a doctor quickly.

'Hello,' she said as she looked at Ben and then me. She carefully examined Ben. 'Sorry if my stethoscope is a bit cold,' she said to Ben before sending us to get his chest X-rayed. 'I'll see you in a bit,' she said to me and Ben. I texted James to tell him where we were. 'Just tell me if I need to come home,' he replied as Ben and I waited to be called through. Ben was coughing miserably, yet weakly because he doesn't have the muscles to do any more. Back in A&E, the doctor returned to say the X-ray was clear but the level of oxygen saturation in his blood was low and Ben's chest sounded crackly.

'I'm assuming you don't want to stay in hospital if you don't absolutely have to?' she asked, as she looked carefully at Ben, noting his breathing. 'I'm guessing staying overnight is complicated because you'd need to go and get loads of stuff?'

'Yes', I said, 'correct. I'd much rather be at home.'

She suggested we go home with a prescription for antibiotics and wait 24 hours. 'If he's not improving then start the antibiotics. I think you have the right instincts so do what you think is best. Bring him back here if you are at all worried. Is that OK?' she asked me. I agreed.

'Bye, Ben, I hope you feel better soon,' she said before moving on to the other patients waiting for treatment.

We returned home and I started the antibiotics the following evening as Ben was not improving. By the time James returned home Ben had recovered. The approach of the A&E doctor was similar to that taken by all of the consultants Ben sees regularly. They talk to Ben. They look at him closely because they want more information than just what they get from X-rays or heart rate monitors. When we leave an encounter with a doctor like this I feel reassured that they have treated Ben as an individual and that I am doing my best to interpret the symptoms of a child that cannot tell me anything about how he feels.

It seems ironic that Ben has such a rich appreciation of language and yet some people assume he understands nothing of what they say. The use and intonation of words is one of the main ways we entertain Ben – we make him laugh by repeating rhymes and we play games where we name objects we can see for him to spot. He loves hearing words and being spoken to. I don't want to mollycoddle him but I also instinctively want to protect him from the realization that stories and words can be hurtful instead of joyful. I want him to assume people want to communicate with him, not realize that some people don't.

All this bubbles away in the back of my mind as we visit a bookshop. I'm with Max and he points out a book by an author we have read before. Her books are short picture books with bold graphics and amusing moments. Max suggests we buy it and I agree because I'm an absolute sucker for books.

Later, I sit on the sofa and suggest we read the new book: *Poo Bum* by Stephanie Blake. Ben is next to me in his chair, Max sits on the sofa on the other side and Molly fidgets around on my lap as I start the story about a rabbit who can only say 'poo bum' and gets eaten by a wolf. His doctor dad realizes he's inside the wolf and retrieves his precious 'poo bum' and the boy rabbit says, 'Good heavens, Father: How dare you call me that! You know perfectly well my name is Simon.'

All three children burst out laughing but Ben carries on laughing the longest and finds it so funny that he does what James calls the 'nose twitch', when he's laughing so much that he stops making any noise. He has a broad smile and scrunched up eyes and the only way you can tell that he's laughing hysterically rather than frozen is that his nose twitches up and down. It lasts a few seconds before the sound of chuckles reappears and then he quietens down. The nose twitch is the holy grail of amusement for Ben. 'Again! Again!' Molly and Max shout and I read the book for a second time. Sometimes I'm considering the careful use of particular words and tone, sometimes I'm policing other people's language and sometimes I'm just shouting 'Bum!' at my kids.

12

I get the kids to bed and sit on the sofa eating dinner and watching TV on my own because James is out. It's winter so it's dark outside and I have drawn the curtains. I have Ben's video monitor with me and I can see he is still awake, moving his arms and shaking his head. I put the monitor down next to me with the volume up. I am so attuned to the sound of Ben going to sleep and the unremarkable noises he makes that I needn't watch the screen to know if he's OK.

Despite the background rumble of recorded waves hitting the shore from the monitor, I hear an unusual noise. I pick it up and see on the little illuminated screen that Ben is gagging and struggling to breathe. This is not unusual but it means there's a reasonable chance he is going to be sick. As I watch to see whether he needs my help, I see a little light appear just above the side of Ben's bed. The room is very dark so it is hard to make out, but Max's little book-reading lamp is illuminating his own face as well as Ben's as he stands at the side of the bed, saying, 'You're OK, Ben. Breathe, Benben. Remember to breathe.'

Ben inhales deeply and coughs. His breathing returns to normal and he is OK. The light disappears. I carry on watching them, just in case, and a few minutes later Ben gags again. Up pops the light and Max's dimly lit face telling Ben, 'Breathe, Benben. It's OK, Ben. You'll be all right.'

I can hear myself in Max's words. He is mimicking what James or I would say if we were standing at the side of Ben's hospital-style bed, raised high to suit our backs. Max hasn't dropped the bed side like we would because the mechanism is too difficult for a six-year-old, but he can just about peer over the top if he stands on his tiptoes. He sleeps on a bed on the floor next to Ben so he is close, as he asked to be.

Ben is still unsettled. Max is so gentle, comforting and mature that I can't bear it. I run upstairs – fast enough but not as fast as I do when Ben is actually vomiting – push open the door and pretend I haven't been watching them talking. 'Is everything OK?' I ask breezily. Max tells me Ben is feeling sick but he has stopped gagging. I check him and then say goodnight again. I watch Ben go to sleep on the monitor downstairs.

I forget to tell James about it for a few days, and once I remember I tell the story to him, Maddy and both grandmothers within a week. Everyone I tell gets tears in their eyes and I too get a tingle in the back of my throat – not because Ben was suffering but because bearing witness to Max being so solicitous to Ben's needs makes my heart want to explode.

Max was calm that night because he'd seen Ben gag before. Possibly hundreds of times. It is not unusual and Max knows that it's likely to be OK. He used to be terrified of Ben vomiting and would run to hide in another room when it happened but now he has got used to it. I don't like that he has had to adjust to such things. Max was being helpful because he's a good brother and he has a sense of responsibility. I don't know how much of that is a typical relationship between a nine- and a six-year-old, and how much is because Ben is disabled.

Max's friend Mia comes to visit for a playdate. They are both six. As I walk with them to our house, the kids cheerfully talk about their day and I tell them Ben will be at home when we get back. 'Is that your dog?' Mia asks.

I am surprised – Mia has been to parties at our house with Ben and I thought she knew him – but I remind her Ben is Max's older brother and goes to a different school because he is disabled. Mia seems shocked. When we arrive home we have a brief chat with Ben and Mel before they go upstairs to Ben's room, and Max suggests he and Mia go and bounce on the trampoline. Mia isn't keen and, after a miserable few minutes with Mia tearfully watching Max bounce, I persuade them to go up to Max's room at the top of the house instead. 'Let's take Lego up there,' I say. Mia is still upset and no amount of jollity about toys or food will calm her. I think perhaps she'd be better alone with Max so I head out of the room to cook dinner. 'Can you close the door?' Mia asks as I go. 'I'll leave it open so I can hear you when I'm downstairs,' I say.

'But you need to shut the door so Ben can't come in,' Mia says.

'Um, no. We are not shutting the door, this is Ben's house,' I say. 'But he's not coming up, he's doing physio downstairs.'

I could shut the door but I won't. Mia is inconsolable now and I can't leave to cook their dinner. I phone Mia's dad who comes to get her. When he arrives, he comes upstairs and calms Mia down. I don't specifically mention any issues with Ben. We all go into the playroom and Mia and Max play happily while Ben is in his bedroom next door, until Ben walks towards the doorway – slow, careful, effortful walking, being supported by Mel and Sarah, his physio. Mia leaps across the room into her father's arms and cowers. He doesn't say anything. 'Great walking, Ben,' I say. 'Well done!'

When Mia leaves, Mel asks if I am OK and I feel dazed. I phone James and factually describe the last few hours to him. As I am describing it I articulate my shock to myself. We have never experienced a reaction to Ben even slightly like this. How do you react to a child being apparently scared of your son because he is disabled? I am pretty sure Ben didn't realize what was going on because he was so focused on walking. I can't tell how much Max understood of why Mia was so upset. Later that week I talk to Max broadly about how some people don't know any disabled people and don't realize there is nothing to be frightened of. I hope this has been a single, unfortunate incident. James and I agree Mia won't come over again.

But it does not go away. This incident becomes a difficult thread that winds through the following months. I can't stop thinking about it. I want to acknowledge what a strange incident it was but when I initiate unsatisfactory conversations with Mia's dad, I don't feel like it's been resolved. I want to make sure it won't happen again. I think often about how children react to difference and wonder how a child can be so scared of someone unfamiliar. I blame myself for taking against a six-year-old. I try to move on, while finding ways to avoid Mia's parents in the playground. I think maybe we are lucky this hasn't happened before. Perhaps this is to be expected with a child like ours?

We encourage discussion at home and we talk often about what Ben is good at and what he finds difficult. We talk about what Max can do that Ben can't: talking, walking, eating. Max brings toys to show his brother and stands up to talk to him in his bed. He knows how to ask Ben questions and watch for whether Ben is looking at 'Yes' or 'No' to reply. He knows what TV programmes Ben likes and will save some chocolate because he thinks Ben would like a taste. Max appreciates that visiting popular museums and theme parks is better with Ben because we get to jump the queues. Sometimes Max talks about it being difficult that Ben is disabled – that he takes up our time and we can't always do things we'd like as a family. Max also complains that Molly is incredibly annoying because she's three and destroys his Lego models. He mainly wants to talk about space, skateboarding and ice cream. Having a disabled brother is one aspect of his life and rarely the most pressing thing on his mind. He is unself-conscious about Ben being his brother and if we lose that I don't know if we'll ever get it back.

As I walk home on an autumnal afternoon with Max and his friend Alex, they talk to me about their day and the games they like. One thought leads to another and then Max says, 'Mia doesn't like Ben.'

'Did Mia say that?' I ask.

'Yeah, Mia told me,' Max says, looking up.

'That isn't very kind,' I say.

'Yeah, and Mia doesn't even really know Ben, does she?' Alex adds.

I see that the thread is still winding its way through our lives, almost a year after Mia's visit to our house. Ben is largely oblivious, protected, but Max cannot escape. What started at home has now flowed through to Max's school – one of the few places where Max is wholly himself and not known as Ben's brother.

That evening, I speak to Max about how wrong this is. 'No one is allowed to be mean about your brother to you, particularly when they don't even know him,' I say, and he listens but is quiet. I ruminate over what to do and a few weeks later I speak to Max's teacher in a rush of sadness and inarticulate thoughts. He reacts with the exact mixture of quiet outrage and disappointment that I need and says he will speak to all of the children about difference and kindness.

A month later, at home over the Christmas holidays with the fallen leaves now swept away, Max comes to me in tears saying he is upset that Mia doesn't like Ben. That thread keeps winding through. We talk again about how it is impossible for Ben to hurt or offend Mia with actions or words so she cannot possibly dislike him. I am calm and clear with Max but raging to myself.

By January, I am determined. As I walk to pick Max up in the early afternoon, with the light already fading, I feel nervous but fierce, like a bear protecting her cubs. I had promised Max I would deal with this. When I see Mia's mum in the playground I say hello. 'This is going to be a difficult conversation,' I say in a rush, 'but I need to talk about something.' I set out the recent insult and link it back to the visit to our house now a year ago. 'Nothing like this has ever happened to us before,' I say hotly. 'I won't let Max hear people say these things about his brother.'

She is shocked and apologizes. She explains that she thought the issues from last year had been resolved and promises to talk about it with Mia and do what she can to make sure it doesn't happen again. 'Thank you,' I say, my controlled rage dissipating and my awkwardness returning. I feel like I am deflating after having puffed myself up to defend my territory.

I tell the latest instalment of the story to my friend Hannah, who has two daughters of similar ages to Ben and Max. Her eldest daughter, Frankie, has autism, developmental delay and health complications so is very different from Ben but the dynamics of our families are similar. I had told her about the first part of the saga when it had happened and she had been angry on Ben's behalf. When I update her on my conversations with Mia's mum, Hannah tells me about a recent conversation she'd had with her youngest daughter, Grace. They had been talking about kids who are different, who are disabled, and

Grace was indignant at Ben being included in the same group as her sister. 'Ben isn't annoying like Frankie,' Grace said to her mum. 'Isn't that funny?' Hannah said to me. 'To Grace, Ben is barely disabled because it doesn't affect her, but to Mia he is probably the most disabled child she's ever met.' We wonder, again, how Ben's disability could have become so intimidating.

I want Max to think of Ben's disability as one of many facets of our family. I hope he sees that although some aspects are made difficult by it, Ben's disability is not inherently bad or sad. I want to preserve Max's protectiveness of his brother, his feeling of solidarity and love, but I don't want it to tip into feeling like an onerous responsibility to him. I want a thread of kindness to run through all that we do. Perhaps I can counteract some people's tendency to fear or pity Ben by filling our family with love and joy. I will not let anyone be unkind to or about Ben. I will unpick their ignorance until they can see that they can be open and generous and all the better for it.

I wonder whether it is my family's role to introduce disability to others or if it is their responsibility to broaden their own horizons. Who should teach children about things that they are not and the people they may not yet have met? Can we teach our children to react to unfamiliarity with kindness?

In the early summer, Max's friend Jack comes to play at our house. They run out to the trampoline in the garden and bounce so much I can hear their jubilant shrieking from inside the house. Sometime later I hear them giggling to themselves, in a way that can only mean mischief. When they call me into the hall it is to witness them pushing Ben's enormous red physiotherapy ball – which is big enough for a nine-year-old to lean against while standing – down the stairs. They let go of it at the top and the huge, outsize ball, bounces down to the front door like a comedy version of bowling. Max and Jack can't stop laughing.

When I eventually persuade them to take the ball back, they can barely push it because it's so unwieldy. I get it upstairs in the lift and together they wrangle it out onto the landing, squeezing it through the doorway to Ben and Max's room with an audible pop, and then pushing it back towards the window. Ben is with Sarah doing physiotherapy so he's lying on a mat on the floor but the boys' enthusiasm cannot be restrained and they roll the ball right over Ben to where it belongs. Ben is unhurt and amused. Molly is shouting at them, 'You squashed my brother!' Ben laughs. Max and Jack ignore everyone and rush off to make rockets out of Lego, and it is all exactly as it should be.

It can feel like there is a gulf between what goes on in our house and what we see beyond. I have become so used to not seeing children like Ben represented in most of the culture we consume. The kids' television channel CBeebies is good at including disabled children but once Ben is a bit bigger and we're not watching it as much, the number of disabled children we see on TV decreases. I actively seek out books, films, art and toys that portray disability positively, or even neutrally, and it's a constant challenge but I am determined. We have a teddy bear with a feeding tube and a toy school bus that is wheelchair accessible. Prudence buys Molly's doll a wheelchair and I buy every book I see with a wheelchair-using character. We have stories about children with autism and feeding tubes and all kinds of difference in an effort to increase the representation our kids see.

Ben is off school one day when he's nine, too ill to go out but well enough to need entertainment, and I start reading him a new book. I get a jolt when the main character, Jessie, talks in the first few pages about her 'lousy palsy' getting in the way of her climbing. *The Ghost of Grania O'Malley* by Michael Morpurgo is a magical story of ghosts, pirates and treasure set against family tensions and the potential destruction of a natural landscape. I feel a little fizz of recognition – I didn't realize this book had a character with disability and it's rare for me to unexpectedly find portrayals like this. Jessie laments her hands not doing what her brain tells them to but also hates her teacher for saying her writing is like a 'demented spider'. She gets into an argument at her school and a horrible girl screams, 'Cripple! My mum says you shouldn't be allowed in the same school with us. They should send you away so's no one's got to look at you.'

I edit the passage as I read to Ben. I don't say 'cripple' out loud but I do read most of the following sentences. I am torn. I don't think Ben knows that word and I don't want to teach insults to him. But it's better for Ben to come across these ideas in fiction, presented as outrageous and mean, than come across them in real life, unprepared. I'm hoping nothing like this ever happens to him but it's inevitable he is going to come across attitudes and words that are hateful. He hears people ask us, 'What is wrong with him?' and tell us they feel sorry for him and us. So I think I have to talk openly about other people's ignorance.

Later in the story, Jessie is lying in front of bulldozers, protesting. 'Jessie stood up – and that took some time. She had to turn herself on to her stomach and push herself up, first on to her knees and then on to unsteady legs.' It is a description of the reality of moving a body that is wobbly that I have never read in a book. I read the book to Ben almost all day until Max and Molly return from school and nursery and disturb us, but we finish it. It's an entertaining story of magic and triumph over adversity, but it's also about impairment, aids and allies. Like all good books, it raises themes beyond the story of Jessie.

Shortly after, I have a conversation with a friend about the books Max and her daughter choose to read, now they can pick up almost any book and have a go. Her daughter has been getting anxious about some of the stories she has been reading, where children face huge peril, but also wants to finish them. Max has started reading some books we have for Ben at home and asking questions about bullies and revenge. It has made me wonder how much we should control what our kids read. Ben only gets to choose books from the options we give him but part of childhood is reading books that are slightly scary, introducing new concepts, seeing that people survive adversity. We know Ben comes across difficult, potentially hurtful, comments. We know he hears people say things that I wish he didn't. Is it good for us to give Ben and his siblings a context into which they can place unacceptable behaviour when they come across it? How much must I awkwardly introduce prejudice in order to prepare them and how much can I ignore it – particularly words like 'cripple' – and hope it never happens to my kids?

When he is nine, I take Ben to a hydrotherapy pool for an immersive theatre performance by the theatre company we love, Oily Cart. It's at an unfamiliar school and there is a teaching assistant on hand to help get Ben and another child ready. As I move Ben onto the changing plinth, the assistant says she will start getting him undressed while I change into my swimming costume. This seems sensible since I can't really get naked in a room full of strangers, but she hasn't introduced herself to Ben so I do this and explain to him I will just leave briefly to get changed. When I come back, Ben is crying because I left and I take over with him but as I put some of his clothes in our bag, the assistant starts to undress Ben's bottom half. 'Don't worry, I'll do that,' I say, but she continues to help. 'You don't need to do that. I can do it,' I say, more firmly. She is being helpful but it feels uncomfortable. I am there and happy to do it. We don't need help. Ben doesn't know her and there is an intimacy to undressing which feels odd with someone who he has just met, who he has only been cursorily introduced to and who he is now expected to be on intimate, but unequal, terms with.

Ben will always require assistance, he will need people (mostly non-disabled) to help him access the world and keep him fed, hydrated and clean. There is likely to be an imbalance in power in these relationships where Ben is more dependent. In a world that prizes individuality and independence above all things, the notion of being dependent is seen as a kind of failure even though no human is successful, or happy, without connections with other people. We are all interdependent. The solution isn't for me or James to do everything for Ben, for us to reduce his dependence on other people by increasing his dependence on us as parents. But I think about how my other children interact with adults – I don't make them do anything they don't want to with strangers. I don't force them to be close to anyone they don't want to be and they wouldn't be undressed by someone they had just met. I am teaching them that they have autonomy over their own bodies and get to choose how it is treated. Ben has a necessarily more personal relationship with people who aren't in his family and I try to work out how to frame these interactions in an age- and impairment-appropriate way. All children are dependent on adults in some way – but Ben needs more help than a typical child and he will continue to need this help into adulthood. We need to establish a way of mediating these encounters now so he knows what to expect as he gets older.

As a bare minimum, it's reasonable for Ben to expect people to introduce themselves and explain or ask him about what's going to happen before they assist him in any way. Sometimes there is chemistry – there are people whom Ben immediately likes and trusts – but we can't expect that this connection will materialize in every interaction. Sometimes Ben's immediate need overrides his lack of warmth to the person doing the changing, feeding or moving. Children don't get to choose all of the adults who they interact with and Ben has less choice and more exposure than most, but I think he should have a sense of what is OK and what is not. He should always feel safe and respected.

A lot of it comes down to building rapport. Some assistants or carers who have spent a lot of time with disabled children come to see the task in front of them (changing into swimming costume) more clearly than the person wearing the swimming costume (Ben). I don't know how we should calculate the pay-off. How much rapport do we need to see between Ben and a carer before we are comfortable with them helping him, or more importantly how awkward or vulnerable is it acceptable for Ben to be if he needs immediate assistance and no one else can provide it?

When Ben and I go into the pool together on this day there are three performers and one other child with his carer, with instruments made out of tubes, floating mirrors and colanders as fountains. It's inventive and I'm thrilled that Ben has this opportunity to experience such an explosion of creativity, but also pleased that I was there to interrupt an encounter that didn't feel right.

Around the same time, we have a new carer at home on some days, Jennifer. She doesn't have a rapport with Ben but, with a full family schedule, she helps ensure Ben has what he needs and is read some books while we ferry the other two kids around. Stories are meant to be our failsafe with Ben but good stories rely on communication and connection and in her hands they are dreary. 'Make sure you chat to him in between feeding him, Jennifer,' I say cheerfully in an attempt to encourage a better relationship between them, though Ben looks unimpressed and I know he doesn't really like her. I feel guilty that he is spending time with her (albeit only a few hours) rather than me.

One afternoon, I go upstairs to see how Ben is getting on and as I walk into his room Jennifer is hoisting him out of his chair in a way that is wrong, despite having been shown how to do it properly. I then realize that she hasn't moved him all afternoon. 'Oh, he needed changing hours ago. Poor Ben!' I say, shocked. The routine on this day has been exactly like other days she has spent with Ben. 'This can't happen,' I say in front of Ben. 'It's not good enough. Can you just leave us for a moment?' I apologize to Ben and change him before putting on an audiobook and stepping outside where Jennifer is waiting on the landing. 'You were in charge of him this afternoon and you didn't change him. You moved him in a way that is dangerous. If you're not sure what you are doing you need to ask us,' I say. My upset is turning to anger and she isn't as apologetic as I need her to be for failing to look after my son, so I ask her to leave. I then bathe Ben carefully and put him in dry, clean clothes. I talk to him gently and then sit with him, Max and Molly while they have dinner and watch a film. I try to heal the upset with the most ordinary evening.

I had reacted in the moment. I felt guilty for having left Ben with her and it seemed as though Ben's vulnerability had been taken advantage of. We generally try to have conversations with Ben's carers away from the children as we don't want our house to be a constant management exercise witnessed by them and they need to have relationships with carers independently of us. I try to respect the professionalism of the people we employ and give them feedback in private. But in this case I didn't regret Ben having witnessed my shock and to know that I thought it was unacceptable. It is not right for Ben to feel physically vulnerable in his own house as he is lifted high above his chair. He can't tell us he feels unsafe so it is our responsibility to make sure he never is. The people who help him with his personal care must give it the thought and attention it deserves because he is dependent on them to help. He shouldn't have to put up with mediocre communication and monosyllabic conversation. I can't control Ben's need for care, but I can choose how it is delivered.

I think Ben should see us standing up for him. We need to make explicit what our expectations are and to hopefully build in Ben a sense of what he can expect from adults, how much he has to put up with and when he's allowed to protest.

We have had a lot of carers work with Ben as there is inevitable turnover when people move away or get new jobs. Mel and Lucy both leave when Ben is eight and we are all sad. Ben had seen Lucy most weekends for two years and Mel five days a week for over a year. When they leave, Ben is subdued and then asks, 'Where…Mel' on his eyegaze device.

Max and Molly talk about Mel and Lucy frequently, asking when we will next see them. They, with Rebecca, Christina, Luke, Beatrice, Rose, Lydia, Sofia and others, were really good at what they did and Ben trusted them. I feel the weight of responsibility for introducing these people into my children's lives, knowing that if they are good then all three children will be upset when they leave. Just as I also feel the burden of the children spending time, in their own house, with people who they don't feel a connection with.

In between the brilliant people, we have other carers where it doesn't work and having them around feels heavy and inconvenient, stressful even. It suddenly feels weird having a stranger witnessing mundane but intimate family moments or sitting at the breakfast table but not eating breakfast. I feel self-conscious dancing with my kids in the kitchen. It doesn't work out with those carers who see Ben as a sequence of needs to be met and not a boy within a bustling family. I find myself saying to them, 'Please can you talk to Ben while you are with him, don't just feed him or move him without telling him what you are doing?' And then later, 'When he is watching TV, can you watch it with him and talk to him about the programme? Please don't just sit next to him on your phone.' Or, 'Perhaps you could read Ben a book. I think he's been watching TV for two hours.'

What I mean is: please make me feel less guilty that you are with my son instead of me. Please make me feel like you are making his day better, not killing time until you leave. Let me believe that you're here for *my* child, not just any old child, and that he likes you. Talk to him like he's a person and make him feel like you care what he thinks. Chat to him about something that isn't essential, or transactional, or the bare minimum.

I am mostly grateful that we have the funds to afford carers to help with Ben but sometimes I feel like I never wanted lots of strangers in my house who I need to train and manage. It is a difficult job that we are asking people to do and we don't always get it right.

Mothering is about showing up, putting in the hours of comforting and wiping. It's about being in A&E at midnight and school runs, reading books and pushing buggies or wheelchairs in the rain. Through all of this you think you are teaching your kids to be good people, showing them how to navigate the world and enjoy themselves, but slowly you realize they are the educators and none more than Ben. Through being there, day after day, meeting the therapists, turning up for the appointments, at school pickups and bedtimes, I develop a depth of knowledge of my children that no one else has. And the flip side of this innate knowledge of Ben is that I have to protect him, from all of the obvious risks to life and limb, but also from people who I thought would be friendly. I sift through the words or actions in any given situation and trust my instincts. If something doesn't feel right then I'll do something about it. For all of the kids, but especially for Ben who can't articulate his discomfort. I use my words in place of his, because words have power.

I think often of how times of adversity change us. My grandmother was widowed young and then raised three sons on her own while trying to make ends meet. One of her sons had three daughters, one of whom, me, had three children. The repetition is pleasing but, more importantly, I hope that personality flows through those bloodlines. She was an optimist, cheerful to the last despite a life of challenges. I hope all of her grit dwells deep in my soul and will bloom in my children. That Ben's brain may have glitches, but his DNA is unaffected and within it is her legacy. I hope all of her good humour and grace in the face of adversity resides in us all and will make itself known, because Ben is going to need all of it. He has physical difficulties, and those we can mostly help him with, but perhaps the attitudes of other people will be the greatest challenge of all.

13

'This is Ben. He is playing the iPad,' the compère says as he gestures towards Ben on the stage. He is one of five children, all using wheelchairs, who are waiting with their instruments ready to play. Beside each of them stands a professional musician poised to start. 'This is Ahmed and he's playing the drum.' Each pupil is introduced before the music begins.

This is the culmination of weeks of work between Ben's school and the London Symphony Orchestra. The musicians have been writing new music in workshops with Ben's class and now they are going to perform it for us. We don't know what to expect. When it comes to Ben's turn, a teacher holds the iPad in front of Ben and he presses on the screen with his clenched hand. A clear note is played. How he moves his hand determines the noise the iPad makes through a speaker. A trumpeter stands directly in front of him and mimics the music from the iPad, creating an analogue–digital duet between the two. Ben is concentrating, we can see from his tense expression, and he succeeds in moving his arm. He is coping with the pressure that we know he will be feeling, as well as the noise from the man playing a trumpet less than a metre from his ears. It is wonderful. I had not expected it to go this well.

Until a few weeks before this performance, when Ben was nine years old, we thought Ben was unable to take part in evening events put on by the school. They have an annual awards night celebration and each time we had taken Ben we had left abruptly with him crying, cheeks flushed with high emotion, overwhelmed by the loud noise and the pressure to appear on a stage. One year, we wheeled him straight off the stage, distraught, out of the building and to our car, leaving all of our extended family in the hall to watch children they didn't know. So we stopped taking him to awards night and had said no to him being included in the LSO concert the previous year. It was too stressful for all of us and I didn't want to subject Ben to occasions that were so obviously not fun for him. We still got the award certificates which we put on the wall above his bed and when we showed them to visitors Ben would smile broadly, pleased with himself.

But we had tried again with awards night this year and it had been better. We talked to him about it a lot in the run-up. As we waited for it to start, James sat next to Ben, furiously reading him Michael Rosen poems to distract him from the noisy people around us. Ben shouted to complain occasionally, finding the unfamiliar hubbub difficult to cope with as people took their seats. As the first class went up onto the stage we saw his bottom lip begin to protrude – the prelude to him crying. But he was also willing to let himself be reassured by James's reading.

When it came to Ben's class's turn, James pushed him to the side of the stage. We had discussed before that Max would join them. Max told Ben jokes while they waited (James told me later they were jokes about death but he decided it wasn't the moment to object). Then a teacher announced Ben's name and achievements – 'For his literacy skills and his growing ability to recognize digraphs when reading and working on his device' – and they went up onto the stage. At the moment that the headteacher offered Ben his certificate they posed for a photo and, with James just behind his wheelchair and Max squished into him on one side, I saw Ben's tense mouth move into a hint of a smile. Just for a second. His cheeks were as flushed as they always are at these events, betraying the level of anxiety Ben was feeling, but there were no tears. I was apprehensive, waiting for the moment that it might all fall apart, but so proud of his determination to get through it.

Then James wheeled Ben off and they disappeared for a class photo. Max reappeared asking for sweets, our bribe to get him through the evening. When James and Ben returned to our seats a little later, we agreed we shouldn't push our luck given Ben's increasingly agitated demeanour and we headed home.

James whispered to me in the car that he was worried they were both going to cry by the time he got Ben off the stage because expectations and emotions had been running so high, for everyone. Ben was visibly pleased with himself. We were relieved. It was such a clear demonstration of progress for him to be able to make it onto the stage and receive his reward for all his hard work at school. It was lovely to see him up there, having his moment, demonstrating all of the determination that had got him this far in life as well as school.

This glimmer of hope had led to us agreeing to the LSO performance. We already knew Ben liked music – at home and in the car he enjoyed the *Hamilton* soundtrack at full volume. The question was whether he could cope with the apprehension and unpredictability of a live performance – but here we are, listening to Ben play the iPad.

Unlike the awards night, we haven't been at all involved in the preparation. Ben's teachers and teaching assistants have looked after all the children after school and all James and I have done is turn up ten minutes before the 7pm performance, say hello to Ben and his friends and take our seats.

For the first 20 minutes, other school children performed and LSO musicians played folk songs. I could see Ben waiting at the side of the stage and I could tell his nose was blocked. Hayfever plus rapid breathing due to anxiety are often a difficult combination for him. Occasionally I heard the snort of him trying to breathe and James and I exchanged anxious looks. A congested nose could derail the evening, but Ben's teacher was sitting next to him, talking to him, spraying his nose with saline, which is what I would have done. She turned his chair away so he couldn't see us and by the time she pushed him onto the stage his nose was clear.

Unlike his first nativity play, which the BBC told me I should have been shocked by but I wasn't, I never imagined this would happen. Until recently, I had wondered if Ben could perform anywhere outside of his Christmas plays without being overwhelmed. But this evening, it feels like not only can he confidently appear in front of the audience, but he doesn't need us. We haven't prepared him for the concert. We haven't talked him through the rehearsal and we didn't help him deal with his blocked nose and mounting anxiety. He had other people to help him with these things.

Watching his relationship with his teacher is a wonder in itself. Motherhood is such a strange combination of interdependency and separation. I can see the gap between us widening. Not a lot, but a little sliver of independence is emerging thanks to his maturity and a school that he loves. As we walk back to the car, people I have never met say goodbye to Ben. 'Well done, Ben, that was great,' a woman says as we pass. 'Who are all these people that know you, Ben?' I ask and he smiles. It has been a remarkable evening.

Whereas once they were regular visitors, these days, our sole engagement with community nurses is to request feeding items – such as syringes or the feeding tube that connects to Ben's button. A few years ago the design of these tubes changed and the tip, where we connect a 'female' syringe onto the 'male' end of the tube, is now made of plastic that glows in the dark. Whenever we go to the cinema and I find the gently glowing end of Ben's tube easily in the gloom, I am grateful to the person whose idea this was and to the system that gets these tubes to us. Recently the tube packets have come with a sticker on the front: 'Please use me for 2 weeks, I cost £15.69 to replace' and I wonder how many of these we have used in Ben's life and what the current balance sheet might be.

But one day, a community nurse visits us at home after school one afternoon, to check Ben is well and to complete an annual review – though I think they forgot to do it last year. She explains that she needs to update the records her team keep on Ben and check that we have the medical supplies we need for him.

I haven't met her before. She is young, with a friendly if uncertain smile and unseasonable ballet pumps that indicate she has driven here. She has printed out a form which is partially complete from their computer records and, as she runs through the different sections, I update her on aspects that have changed: daily medication, how much food and water Ben has, which professionals he sees. We are sitting at our dining table and the kids are upstairs with a new carer, Charlie, though I can hear Molly shouting and Max arguing back. There is a rumble from the kitchen ceiling as Ben's chair is moved across the floorboards above us.

The nurse reads out the next questions from the form: 'How does he communicate? How is his play and development?'

I wonder how relevant Ben's ability to communicate is to the supply of syringes and extension sets but give a brief summary. 'It's complicated,' I conclude. I'm not sure how to summarize his development.

I think of myself as a people pleaser. I want people to like me and I dislike confrontation and social awkwardness. If someone asks me a question, I tend to answer it. I know that I can't always predict what health professionals need to know and why. But I am becoming increasingly comfortable with not answering questions just because they have been asked. The answer to these questions – any questions about Ben's play, development or communication – are highly nuanced. It is complicated terrain. I know Ben isn't playing or communicating in the way that a typical nine-year-old might but he's developed hugely since he was a baby and can now play the iPad with the LSO. His development is delayed, but I don't want anyone to think that means it's inadequate.

Ben is non-verbal but that doesn't mean he can't communicate. He can't speak but he can make noises that are not words. There are different kinds of sounds for happy, sad, interested, annoyed. Even without the noises, I could tell you whether Ben is in pain, bored, excited or frustrated just from the way he moves his body. Not always, but often. I know from his bucking torso, as if trying to move, and his furious looks towards the garden that he wants to go outside. I know from the hint of a wince on his face and the small kick of his hip in his wheelchair that he's in pain. All of these movements are a kind of communication. But also all of his movements can undermine his communication. We can't rely on him shaking his head for no when he often shakes his head in an effort to lift it up. He is unable to point with his fingers because he doesn't have sufficient control of his arms or hands, but he can point using his eyes. His efforts to look at symbols or a screen are consistently undermined by the involuntary movements of his limbs and torso over which he has little control.

Ben can choose the specific audiobook he wants out of a choice of 30 by looking at the 'No' symbol taped to the arm of his wheelchair as we read the first 29 titles and then swinging his eyes to the 'Yes' symbol for the 30th. When we are looking at the communication program on his eyegaze computer and I wonder aloud how to find the word banana he selects the page for 'eat and drink', then 'food', then 'fruit', then 'banana'. If I write four words on scraps of paper and put them in front of him, he can tell me which is 'banana' by looking. If I ask if he wants to eat a banana he looks down at 'No'. When I ask him if he wants to watch TV he'll eye point to 'Yes'. When I ask if he knows that I love him, and I will love him for ever no matter what he does, he answers 'Yes' again.

Yet given a keyboard on his eyegaze device he often doesn't spell words that I know he recognizes. When I ask him if he wants to go for a swim one day he refuses to answer even though I know he loves swimming, and when he goes in the water that day he loves it. His communication is limited and unpredictable. It's hard to put a finger on how he is developing.

When he was seven, I thought he was doing really well because he was communicating with us more, using the software on his eyegaze device to choose appropriate words, but he still didn't reliably answer 'Yes' or 'No' to questions. When he was eight, his 'Yes' and 'No' responses were more reliable but his spontaneous conversation using his eyegaze device was inconsistent. On his ninth birthday, he was using his communication software to say things that were entirely appropriate, choosing and reading stories to himself on his device. Now that he's nearly ten, we are certain that when he answers 'Yes' or 'No' to a question it is meaningful. We ask him whether he wants to sleep on his back or his side when he's in bed and have no doubt about his answer, finally. It's taken five years to get to this level of reliable communication and it has been a slow, unsteady journey. It is sweet, hard won, progress for him.

The timescale of helping Ben learn new skills is long, which means it's hard to know whether he is improving and therefore whether we are doing the right thing. It can feel pointless to continue working on something that appears to be having little impact but he won't learn anything if we allow ourselves to be discouraged when he doesn't make immediate breakthroughs. Progress is subtle and understated because he's learning complex skills involving deft eye control, motor planning, memory and language. Ben first trialled an eyegaze device when he was two. He had more regular access to one when he was four. We bought a laptop with an eyegaze tracker for him when he was five which he used a few times a week. He got an NHS-funded eyegaze device mounted onto his wheelchair when he was seven and then started using it every day at school. Each development gave him more time to practise and it's so far been years of chipping away slowly at the monolith of communication.

Sometimes progress doesn't look how you imagine: Ben goes through periods of navigating out of his communication software every time I try to talk to him with it. In order to avoid communicating with me, he is adept at selecting three different cells in different positions on three different pages on his computer to instead take himself to a game or story on his device. I thought supporting his communication was meant to mean he conversed with me more, but his increasing skill actually results in him refusing to talk to me at all. He is clearly indicating he wants to read (or be read) a book. His skill in navigating around his device is admirable. It's progress. I respect his determination but it's disheartening. To force him to talk in his communication software would be as inappropriate as refusing to let him talk, but I want him to want to tell me things.

I try to remember that I am aiming to give Ben the independence to communicate in his own way, which is different from mine. Talking through assistive technology is not the same as direct speech and I have to alter my habits accordingly. I need to expand my own narrow notion of how conversations work. I find it uncomfortable to leave gaps and feel I have to fill them but it takes time to speak via a device. Ben isn't able to shout immediately, in the way that Max and Molly do frequently, 'Mummy, I was in the middle of talking when you interrupted me!', so I have to check myself. I frequently screw up even when I am trying my best. I realize after a conversation with a woman called Holly who uses a communication aid that I had said goodbye and walked away without waiting to see if she wanted to say goodbye, or even if she had anything else to say. I feel a little sting of shame that night.

If we accept that people with communication difficulties have a right to talk – and therefore to be given the support, equipment and training they need – then they also have the right to be heard. And I have to learn how to listen – to not make assumptions about what is being said, or interrupt, or fill the gaps in conversation with inconsequential waffle, but actually listen. Ben really likes Shel Silverstein poems and we read one entitled 'Deaf Donald'. A woman called Talkie Sue has a conversation with a man, Deaf Donald. She speaks and he signs back. She cannot understand his reply to her asking, 'Do you like me too?' And so, 'She left forever so she never knew that [drawing of Donald signing] means I love you.' Conversations are as much about being able to listen and understand as they are about talking.

As I am trying to learn more about alternative methods of communication, my phone rings when I am in a playground with Molly. When I answer the phone I can only hear muffled noises and I hang up. The same number rings again and when I answer I still can't hear anything but it doesn't feel like a mistake. I wait a moment and I hear an electronic voice saying, 'This is a communication aid. Do not hang up.' I am confused but intrigued and then I hear the voice say, 'Hello, this is Kate,' and I recognize the voice as a disabled woman I know through an augmentative and alternative communication group we have been to. The electronic speech is slow because I realize Kate is using her communication device to speak through the phone and I wait for her to complete her sentence before replying, 'Hi Kate, how are you?' We have a chat – about something she had seen me post online – as Molly moves to a climbing frame nearby. This is a kind of communication to aim for.

Ben will have brief chats with me, mostly in the context of a specific conversation rather than unprompted speech. When my youngest sister Rosie sends him a present for his birthday, I go to the 'special events' page on his device. Ben chooses 'happy' and 'birthday' unprompted. 'This present was from…' I say and I navigate to the 'people' page, where Ben selects 'Rosie'. 'Yes, from Rosie, and look what she's bought you!' I say as I open the box. I open the 'clothes' page on his device as I open the parcel with one hand, stopping to help Molly move away from Ben's kicking feet. As I pull out a pair of trainers with illuminated soles I hear Ben, via his device, say 'shoes'. 'That's right, Ben!' I say, ruffling his hair in celebration. It is everyday speech, years in the making. He can do it, but it's not simple.

There are stories on the internet of mothers – and they are always mothers – who have known deep in their souls that their disabled children have the capacity for communication and literacy but are being failed by the professionals supporting them. These mothers take matters into their own hands and tutor their children at home, painstakingly preparing resources on their kitchen tables and slowly, methodically, teaching their children letters and short words before increasing the syllables and making sentences. They fight for the right equipment and the best support. Their children make dramatic progress and are eventually able to talk about how trapped they felt by being underestimated and misunderstood.

Obviously I want Ben to be the subject of these internet stories – celebratory, happy stories featuring quotes from children that previously couldn't formulate expressive language. They make me question whether Ben has the right communication device or equipment. Is he getting the right education? Is he getting enough specialist input? Should I be homeschooling him? Am I, personally, doing enough to encourage his literacy? Are we modelling his method of communication enough? Are we doing it every day, in every place, at every opportunity? Because that's what the people on the internet are doing and if Ben doesn't become expressively literate I think that it will be my fault.

I don't know if we are doing well or badly at helping Ben communicate and develop. It's hard to find disabled adults who communicate exactly like Ben or other parents of children like Ben. I try to seek them out online. I find out about events, equipment and techniques. I make connections with disabled people, like Kate, learning more about their experiences. What I am particularly drawn to are stories about disabled children overcoming communication difficulties and adults who use assistive technology – devices or symbols to help them talk. It is inspiring to see people who have found the system that works for them and are then able to say what they want to say fluently. It's encouraging to see that methodical, consistent use can pay off – that children who had been unable to communicate now have a viable way to do so. It makes me feel hopeful that all of the work we are putting in with Ben is worthwhile.

I know I don't want to homeschool my children, any of them. I'm not a teacher. I taught in an English summer camp for Spanish kids when I was younger and I learned that I am an impatient teacher who shouts a lot. I think there is huge value in children learning from all kinds of people, meeting other adults who are interesting, knowledgeable, generous and may do things differently to me. Ben loves school – it's a place where he learns, swims, makes friends, goes on trips. I couldn't possibly take all of that away from him. But it niggles at me that Ben doesn't spell out words I know he knows. He has shown me that he can match individual phonic sounds to the letters. He can identify a word out of four when I ask him to. When we write 'table' on a piece of paper and show it to him (without saying anything), he'll eye point to the table. But he won't or can't demonstrate any kind of consistency to his teacher at school and when presented with an eyegaze keyboard, he doesn't spell out words that are easy for him to read. He loves hearing and reading words, but apparently hates spelling them. Late one night I read another account of a child whose potential was unrealized until a eureka moment where they spelled out their thoughts after consistent, bespoke teaching and I worry again that we are failing him.

A good compromise is to find him a tutor. We find Anna and it is one of those times when the stars align and she, a qualified special needs teacher with an interest in literacy, has time to see Ben. We meet her and I can tell Ben likes her, though he doesn't want to do some of the exercises she tries and I spend some of the session encouraging him into it. I think Anna is wondering whether this is going to work and I say, to myself as much as everyone else, 'Let's give it some time!'

Over the next few weeks, Anna sees Ben regularly. Each time she arrives wearing trainers with a heavy bag of resources over her shoulder like she's ready for action. We settle into a rhythm of a weekly session and she works through the phonics alphabet. 'He knows all of the single letter sounds,' Anna says after one session, and plays games where he has to match rhyming words at the next. Sometimes Ben gets grumpy and is uncooperative. Anna rewards hard work by reading a few pages from a book periodically through the sessions, and over the weeks the pages slip by.

We go through another period without a regular carer during the week so James picks Ben up from school on Tuesdays. He walks him to a library where Anna meets them and, once James has given Ben some water and food, he leaves them to it for an hour. The layout of the library means James can keep a surreptitious eye on them while he works but Ben can't see him. Occasionally James sends me surveillance-style photos of Ben and he's mostly looking at Anna or the book she is holding, his involuntary movements stilled by his concentration as he listens to her speak or answers her question. One day Anna explains to James that she's been putting Ben's hand on her throat as she speaks, holding it there because he can't keep it there himself, so he can feel the vibrations of her talking and how the sound changes for different words. She is wondering if it might help him think about the different phonetic sounds, since he cannot make these sounds himself.

How do you learn to talk and write if you cannot speak? Max started talking late. He only said 'mum', 'dad' and 'oh no' as he turned two but had a large vocabulary of words he could understand. 'Are you at all worried about his speech?' his keyworker at nursery asked me and I had to work out how to answer his question sensitively, treading a line between saying I wasn't while not being dismissive. It wasn't that I hadn't thought about it – I had.

By that point I'd spent hours with Ben's speech and language therapists. I knew how early language developed, how you could tell a non-verbal child understood the link between noun and object, then eventually generalize to a symbol representing the object. I had painstakingly taught Ben how to look at the small plastic animals I held in front of him to show me which was which when I said 'giraffe', then how to look at a photo, a drawing, a symbol of the animal, until eventually he could generalize the word 'giraffe' to any version of the tall mammal. I knew that Max had no problems with language – he could identify a depiction of a giraffe in any setting without any specific training – he was just taking his time. When a health visitor came to visit us to discuss it she said, 'He clearly knows a lot of words' and Max pointed at my nose. 'Oh, he knows nose!' she said laughing.

Within three months of his second birthday, Max was speaking in three- or four-word sentences. He was fascinated by the world and once he started telling us about it he wouldn't stop. We could see his brain working and his body co-ordinating itself to communicate with an ease and fluidity that was beautiful to watch and hear. We could understand most of what he said and all of those words which he had been storing up before he turned two came tumbling out, but not quite accurately. He confused the L, W and R sounds and this continued until he was four. We tried to help him understand the difference, how the glide of tongue and lips changed for these letters, but he just got annoyed with us. He was confused when people couldn't understand him and occasionally embarrassed when they turned to us to check they had heard correctly. I would correct their misunderstanding, not at all self-consciously, because correcting a mispronunciation was the least of our family's communicative challenges.

When I asked one of Ben's speech and language therapists about it she said it was common. 'No one will worry about it until he's five,' she said. She told me it's called gliding when these kinds of sounds are replaced; therapists would say he was replacing a liquid (r, l) with a glide (w). When Max started school we mentioned it to his teachers and they weren't concerned. 'We see it all the time,' they said. 'Let's wait and see if he still does it when he's learned those

phonics sounds.'Through that reception year he learned the
letter sounds and the accompanying actions and songs and
we gradually noticed that he was now clearly talking about
'licking lollipops' and 'Awert!' became 'Alert!' His brain had
matched up the sounds he had heard with the muscles in
his tongue and mouth. His mouth could now make sounds
that were liquid when they needed to be, and solid where
appropriate.

We think Ben has a glitch in this loop of learning. Like
Max, he has been taught the letter sounds, what they sound
like and how they are written. He has seen how they make
words. He is learning whole words too. But we can't know
how he hears any of it in his head since he can't speak. There
is no way of knowing whether his brain is making sounds that
are liquid or not as we can't hear them, and nor can he. There
is no feedback loop for him. The only solution is to work on
communication techniques and keep teaching him letters,
words and language in the hope that at some point they come
together into expressive literacy. I don't have an endpoint in
mind, I just want to feel like we have done everything we can
and hope to see little incremental moments of progress.

It's hard to summarize Ben's communication or development
into a neat little answer like the community nurse hoped for. It's
not black or white, it's a massive swathe of grey. I don't want to
risk downplaying his progress by simplifying his skills but nor
do I want to overstate his abilities. Some people look at Ben
and assume he cannot communicate at all. Others are so keen
to presume Ben's competence that they will seize any reports

of progress with a certainty and enthusiasm which makes me uncomfortable. I wonder whether their joy is based on a lack of ambition – are they amazed at his brilliance because they assumed he couldn't do it? Then I feel bad for being so cynical. What is the right balance between expecting your child to achieve and being pleased when they do? If you're too jubilant maybe it looks like you never thought it would happen in the first place. It means I am cautious about sharing moments of success, not least because I know that whatever he has done might not be repeated next week. It's a winding path.

After three months of them working together, I come into the room as Anna and Ben are finishing a session and she says he has done well. 'His reading is good. He read this book on his own,' she says holding up a slim kid's book, 'using his internal voice. I just turned the pages,' she says. 'I then asked him questions about the story and he got them all right.' I feel like this is vindication of my estimation of his abilities. Anna has been working Ben out, not underestimating him but waiting for him to show her what he knows before making assumptions. He thrives with this kind of attention and expertise – people who take him seriously, who have expectations underpinned by empathy, who aren't just comfortable with the challenging terrain of his kind of learning but are embedded in it. Anna listened to what we told her – 'He knows letter sounds! He can read!' – but waited until she had seen it for herself to confirm. She isn't amazed, but she is pleased.

Almost all the skills Ben has mastered so far have been underpinned by the support and expertise of professionals who are really good at what they do. Physiotherapists, occupational therapists, speech and language therapists, teachers, teaching assistants, carers who put the hours in. Breakthroughs aren't made in a one-hour clinic appointment, they are gained through regular, consistent effort by Ben and the people helping him. The best people are clearly focused on what will suit him best – they aren't precious or ideological but are problem solvers.

One morning, Anna joins a visit at home by Ben's speech and language therapist. As they are looking at Ben's eyegaze device together they discuss whether his head control, and therefore his control of where his eyes point, would be improved by him holding onto something. We don't have anything suitable as he sits at our dining table, so they each offer him one of their thumbs. For over an hour they work with Ben to give him the best chance of succeeding with his eyegaze device, and he holds onto their two thumbs throughout.

I don't want Ben to be literate so that I can boast about his skills, I just want more insight into his thoughts and his wishes. At a training day, Kate, who I had spoken to on the phone, says, 'People sometimes think of a communication aid as a gift or a toy, that users should feel grateful to have been provided with. Whereas it is in fact a human right.' Helping Ben to find a way to communicate isn't a nice idea, it's the most basic of his rights. I want him to be able to tell me, and others, when he feels sick, what he wants or when we're wrong. As he matures and handles nerve-wracking experiences, like awards night and the LSO concert, with fortitude and bravery I want him to be able to tell us what's changed.

So here we all are. We have pitched our tents on the undulating landscape of uncertainty and we're making the most of it. Mindful of the five years it took for a reliable 'Yes' or 'No' answer to a question, we are ready for the next stage of the journey. We've got our eyes on routes up the slopes. The ground is solid beneath our feet and we know how to find the people to help us. We are all doing our best.

14

'William, intent upon his own thoughts, went out into the garden moving his arms to and from with eloquent gestures and murmuring, "And now, Ladies and Gentlemen, kindly allow me to introduce to you King Charles being hung in the tower by a policeman like what he was in the old days, lifelike and natural, Ladies and Gentlemen..."'

Ben's portable speaker is attached to the handle of his wheelchair and he is listening to Just William stories by Richmal Crompton so we can all hear tales of William and his friends, the Outlaws, roaming the English countryside, getting up to mischief. James, Ben, Max and I are sitting outside a café in Trafalgar Square having lunch towards the end of the summer holiday. There are crowds of tourists heading towards the National Gallery and pigeons pecking at leftover food.

We have just been to the theatre to see *Horrible Histories*. We had perfect seats at the back of the circle, quite a long way from the stage but with a brilliant view. There was no one behind us so we didn't need to worry about Ben's wheelchair blocking their way. The boys have watched almost every episode of the TV programme so we knew what to expect and it was genuinely amusing for all of us: poo jokes interspersed with historical facts, raps about Henry VIII. Ben enjoyed it, though he was dripping with sweat by the end with the nervous energy of coping with unpredictable music and loud actors.

Ben gets bored if he is left unamused for any length of time, with nothing to watch or no one reading to him, so audiobooks have become his entertainment. His constant head movements won't allow him to wear headphones but with an iPod and a wireless speaker we can put on books by David Baddiel, Francesca Simon or Kaye Umansky in any location. It means James and I have the opportunity to eat our sandwiches while feeding Ben. '"Crumbs!" chorused the Outlaws in delight,' says the speaker and Ben laughs as his arms whirl.

When Ben was younger, I would have found a trip like this very daunting – would we be able to get Ben's wheelchair into the theatre? Would we remember everything we needed? Would Ben cope with the performance? I would have felt self-conscious feeding him outside the café and anxious about playing an audiobook for him in case we disturbed anyone with the noise. I might have noticed if people were looking at Ben. Now, I unconsciously screen out his wobbliness, his wheelchair and the apparatus of tube feeding, and don't notice or care whether people look, so as he chuckles and I glance over, all I see is a boy having a really fun day. The people of Trafalgar Square are too busy to notice him.

I spent most of Ben's early life thinking as little as possible about him becoming a disabled adult. I knew he was disabled and that he was a child who was going to grow up. I knew his disability was permanent. But I couldn't bear to think of him as a grown-up because it would mean he was no longer my baby and I might not be able to protect him. I felt like the world would inevitably get harder for him and I wouldn't be able to make it OK. It was easier to remain fixed in the moment where he was a child who was naturally dependent and I could make his life good. I was happy with him going to school, taking him to the activities we knew he liked and getting cross when he was not included. His adult life would be different and it was intimidating. But as I watched him get taller and pull away from me, if not physically then emotionally, I knew I had to start imagining our futures.

In 2015 I saw a show called *Weighting*, by a theatre company called Extraordinary Bodies. It was set up in the middle of a local park on an early evening in May when it was still light and mercifully dry. The performance was centred around a large metal staircase suspended from a tall gantry which was also a see-saw and a bridge. The actors used the staircase to perform incredible acrobatics in a story about a father's fear of letting his daughters go out into the world. They were lit by the sun setting behind us as they climbed, hung and balanced their weight against each other.

The actor playing the father made his way onto the bridge as he came to accept that his family must leave him. I could see echoes of Ben's body in the way he moved. He had some difficulty walking and as he slowly and carefully climbed the steps they tilted under his weight and suddenly he leaped off the edge. Attached to a harness he flew up, suspended high above the ground, looking completely free. He was liberated from the force of gravity on feet and wobbly legs as his character was released from self-imposed restriction. The sheer joy of it was exhilarating.

It was the first time I had seen disabled bodies in such a beautiful way. The cast were not limited by their physical impairments but their disabilities were entwined into a show about hope, love and taking risks. I found it profoundly moving that I was being shown a lead actor whose body had similarities with Ben's in its twists and tone. When I later met him he said, 'I get to fly, which is no longer scary, but brilliant fun.'

I didn't know whether Ben would like to be suspended upside down from an enormous revolving bridge but I wanted him to have the opportunity to find out. If you can't try something then it's impossible to know whether you might like it and surely life is all about trying new things, taking risks both physically and emotionally. It was the start of me feeling less intimidated by the thought of Ben becoming an adult and more excited about the opportunities that might be available to him.

Unless we seek it out, we aren't shown disabled people going on physical adventures or anything of their inner life.

I hadn't been shown disabled people as multi-faceted humans with emotions and experiences separate to their disability. Disabled people in the media are mostly either elite athletes or recipients of charity and/or sympathy. I sought out alternative stories. When I met parents of adult disabled people I became more interested in what their children were doing rather than intimidated by imagining my son that old. I started learning from disabled people about their lives and challenges. I opened my eyes and my ears and was encouraged and emboldened by what I saw and heard.

In a society where people are judged on their ability to be productive and independent, disabled people are often seen as too reliant. Ben's body doesn't conform to what is 'normal' and the difference is seen as wrong. This affects every aspect of life for disabled people, from education to work, from the welfare state to medical care. There is a pervasive sense that disabled people are problems to be fixed, and perceptions are slow to shift. I realize that this is the view that I had when Ben was born. I had some friendships with other parents of disabled children in those early years, and I had lots of discussions with various professionals who worked with disabled children, but it didn't occur to me that it would be possible to make connections with disabled adults. I thought of *my* child as different to *those* disabled adults and it has taken years for me to connect him (and me) to older people with physical impairments. When Ben grows up, their challenges will be his challenges, and their power will be his power.

My belated realizations are necessary but also confronting. I am not disabled and might be part of the problem. Disabled people don't need more people to speak for them but for their own needs to be recognized and their voices amplified. I know a lot about my son, and can advocate for him, but I can't truly know his experience. I had thought disabled people deserved my sympathy but I now know I need to listen and offer my righteous anger and loud voice when it is required.

It seems ironic to me that Ben's body, thought to be inferior or undesirable, is what tells his story. He uses his body, his head, eyes and voice, to communicate. In the same way that I can sometimes tell from the particular sound of his cough whether he needs to see a doctor, I am able to tell whether he is in pain from the particular way he moves his back or how excited he is by how he moves his legs. His body is what makes him disabled but it isn't something to be pitied or dismissed – it is nuanced and precious.

Since 2014, I have been counting the number of appointments Ben has each year – to see doctors, have therapy, get equipment checked, have blood tests – and the number has barely changed. He had 151 appointments in 2014 and he had 146 in 2019. The logistical challenge of being his mother has in some ways changed little and in others a lot. It is still trying sometimes but it feels so different. It's difficult to unpick whether Ben has fewer needs and it's more straightforward being his mother or if I have got better at looking after him and managing my own expectations. Probably both. But being his mother feels lighter and smoother, most of the time.

If there were scales with the weight of Ben's needs on one side and unpressured, enjoyable parenting on the other, the early years were perpetually tipped towards the pressure of his needs. Now they are far more often weighted on the other side, by the unconstrained, delightful moments of being Ben's mother. My days are still often relentless and complicated but that exists side-by-side with joy and fun. I can now acknowledge the complexity of his life and the challenges he and we face while mainly celebrating the person he is and enjoying the opportunity to spend time with him. The two sides are inseparable.

I didn't ask to have a family like mine. I had never given any thought to there being families like the one I found myself in. Having Ben made me different from most of the people around me and for a while I thought that was unlucky but it isn't. Being different is valuable. It may be complicated but it isn't inferior. We have better lives than many.

My husband and I are a team but we rely on other people to help our family as we can't do it all alone. Raising Ben has been a collective endeavour, built on the foundation of our wider family. Not only in genes, but in practical help. We have parents that will drop everything to help us, siblings and their partners who will look after our children whenever we ask, and answer the phone whenever we call. We have been helped by friends, teachers, therapists, doctors, nurses and paid carers.

As he turns ten, Ben has already had 26 carers. Some amazing, some less so, but they have contributed so much to our family. We have carers who have been working for us for years. Beatrice has now been looking after Ben at night, almost every week, for five years. She knows every movement he makes and exactly what TV programmes he likes. Molly has known Rose since she was six months old, as far back as her memory goes. When Rose arrives, Molly and Max tell her their news and they have no sense that she is just there for Ben. At night, she knows instinctively how Ben wants to lie and during the day she can always make him laugh. When Ben is ill she knows how to comfort him. Sometimes when I work I can hear her reading Ben a book and he laughs so much he goes silent (when I know his nose must be twitching) until I hear a great gasp of amusement as he recovers himself. Watching my children form relationships like this, even if they won't last for ever, feels like a privilege.

I don't know what makes us the parents that we are. I wonder how much of my mothering is influenced by my mother, or my grandmother, and how much of me has been made by Ben. I know that the way I mother Max and Molly is deeply influenced by how I have been moulded by Ben: the joy in little fingers eating blueberries; the appreciation of how easily Max and Molly talk. Ben taught me to not make assumptions about children, about respecting their desires or dislikes and aiding their efforts. Perhaps counterintuitively, I think it makes me more relaxed. I am so pleased that the younger two can mostly express their needs, that their bodies are simple and their opportunities near boundless, that I don't get too worried about whether they eat or nap at the same time each day. I want them to eat vegetables but otherwise I am relaxed about their diet. I let them climb to the limit of their physical abilities and wear goggles on their heads to go to nursery (where they definitely won't be swimming) if they want, appreciating that they can put the goggles on themselves rather than dwelling on how eccentric they look. I try to answer their questions as clearly and truthfully as I can, marvelling at their curiosity, not shying away from challenging topics.

I am a member of an invisible club – one of parents quietly learning from their disabled children and then trying to change the world in ways big and small. It is an unashamedly domestic beginning for a political movement, and it's a movement of people who are sleep-deprived, a bit distracted and dealing with complicated logistics. When Ben was little and I was chronically underslept, I often felt overwhelmed but as he's got older, I have emerged from my own little domestic sphere. I am filled with wonder and indignation.

I now view everything through the prism of being Ben's mother and it has made me both more gentle and more angry, more patient and more vociferous. My family is subject to the whims of political decisions and budget restraints. Reductions in funding aren't just abstract concepts to disabled people – they mean less money for people to care for and support Ben and cause the transport to his holiday play scheme to evaporate. There isn't an option to not be politically engaged, and often angry, because Ben relies on the support that the state provides.

I realize that much of parenting isn't carefully orchestrated moves, dramatic decisions or big reveals. Most achievements aren't an end in themselves but the beginning of something else. When we realized Ben was going to survive, it was the beginning of learning how to be his parents. When he started to communicate it was the start of helping him express himself more. Each time, we learn a bit more and push forward on our new path. I am content not despite Ben's impairments but with them. I'm not being heroic, I am just trying to help him stay healthy and do things he enjoys. To improve at skills which will help him get the best out of his days. To make sure he gets the opportunities and support he needs to have fun. To love and be loved.

As we head into winter, we approach Ben's tenth birthday. It has always been a challenge to think of presents he will like, apart from books which we buy him all year round. Ben isn't interested in many toys since they usually need co-operative hands. Over the years, we have bought specially adapted toys, but he's too old for these kinds of presents now and has no interest in watching a ball rotate or penguins toddle up to a slide. We have bought plenty of gifts over the years which were chosen more so I didn't feel bad about his not having many presents rather than because Ben wanted or liked them.

I see a photo somewhere of a big appliqué textile wall hanging and decide I'll make something like this for Ben that can be a bedspread or hung over the end of his bed. I buy a piece of fabric (a cheap, plain tablecloth) and cut out felt letters and shapes to make a pattern. Laying the fabric out on the kitchen table, I pin the felt pieces on before stitching them on with a sewing machine I borrow from Maddy. I haven't used a sewing machine for years and I get frustrated winding the bobbin, threading the machine and getting the tension right. I am slow but steady, like my mum taught me. I have to work on the quilt when Ben is not around so I wait until the kids are in bed before clearing the table and laying out my pieces of fabric. After a week of working in the evenings I am not even half done, so I start to work on it during the day when Ben is upstairs or out, and I swear Molly and Max to secrecy. I enjoy the process of slowly building up the pattern. After ten days of finding an hour or two here or there I have finished the machine sewing and it's not neat but I think the stitches will hold. The next few days I spend carefully threading each loose thread to the back of the quilt before tying them off so that, hopefully, the whole thing won't unravel.

On the weekend before Ben's actual birthday, we have a small tea party with family. My parents bring a present for him – a subscription to a magazine, almost like a book but different – and we put Ben at the head of the table while they read him jokes and he laughs. Maddy, George and their son Ralph arrive with huge red helium balloons: a one and a zero. We put ten candles on the cake which is Harry Potter themed and, as James lights them, we sing 'Happy Birthday' and Ben is smiling at us all. He doesn't find the singing around flames stressful today and he's relaxed. When we have finished our 'hip hip hoorays', Max and Molly blow out the candles for him and I take a piece of the cake next door to blend it up to go through his feeding tube. We all reminisce about Ben's second birthday cake which was egg-free, since Ben is allergic to eggs, but strangely tasted almost exclusively of egg, and how that was the day we first met George, and Max, Molly and Ralph didn't exist, and I marvel at how much has changed.

Ben has never had a birthday party with friends. We have had a little gathering every year with family and close friends. We've had cakes and garlands, songs and presents. Every year James makes a video of Ben's last year and we all watch it together. We instigated a tradition of birthday ice skating. But there's been no big party with school friends and chaos, partly because Ben didn't seem to like parties. He found the number of people and the noise difficult. He didn't enjoy party games with lots of kids and cried when we sang. He didn't have an obvious friendship group in the way Max did – his school has never been local and his classes have been smaller – so it was hard to know who to invite and I found the idea of it stressful.

But ten feels like a milestone to mark. Ben had been invited to a friend's party at an ice rink a few months previously and I was thrilled to realize it's possible to briefly hire an ice rink and so we have organized a tenth birthday party with family and friends, kids from school and home and their siblings.

At the start, we are the only ones there and Ben and James swirl around alone, the entire rink to themselves. Ben's friends arrive and it's a wonderful mix of semi-competent and incompetent skaters offering to push wheelchairs in the interests of their own stability. Molly and her cousin Ralph wobble around holding onto plastic penguins. Max approaches it with admirable confidence, keeping moving to stay warm because I forgot to bring his coat. There are 13 kids on the ice, 6 of them using wheelchairs.

When we finish skating, the kids that can eat help themselves to carbohydrates and sugar and Ben sits happily among them. Then we light candles and sing around some amateur egg-free cupcakes. As we sing, he beams, thoroughly enjoying the noise and the attention. We feed him pre-blended cake as others tuck in. In the unphotogenic surroundings of a local authority ice rink, sat in front of a vending machine, Ben has fun. After ten years we have worked out how to give him a party he enjoys. It's taken time for us to encourage his friendships and for him to come round to the idea of being the centre of attention. It is glorious. He is glorious.

On the morning of Ben's actual birthday, we all come down to the kitchen where we have laid out his presents the night before – not too many, so he isn't overwhelmed, but a few from us, one from a friend and a few from his carers. I have hung the finished quilt at one end of the kitchen table: a big black piece of fabric with colourful letters which reads YES YOU CAN. I am aiming for some kind of hybrid of the positivity of Bob the Builder and the optimism of an Obama presidential campaign. Ben looks at it and smiles, reading the words. I can tell he likes it. Max congratulates me on how good it is, and we open Ben's first present on his lap. I hold it steady while Max and Molly take off the wrapping paper for him. It's a smart speaker and we have programmed phrases into Ben's eyegaze device so he can make it work by talking to it. Taking our cue from Max, one of the phrases we have included is 'Alexa, make a fart noise' and Ben finds this phrase immediately and by choosing this cell on his eyegaze computer he makes the speaker fart. The noise is really disgusting and everyone laughs and he does it again and again.

We all go together to pick up Ben from school that afternoon. Max wanted to come too and since he rarely gets to visit Ben's school we decide he can join us. When Molly and I go to collect him from school he says that he has made Ben a birthday card. His teacher had asked if he wanted to miss PE in order to make something for Ben's birthday.

Max, Molly and I meet James at Ben's school and the kids go into Ben's classroom to find him while James and I wait at the entrance. When Ben emerges he is smiling at us all. At a café round the corner, we meet James's parents for a little celebration. They have presents, even more books, and we have tea and cakes and light an illicit candle (hoping it doesn't trigger a fire alarm). It's a bit noisy and I worry Ben is going to be overwhelmed but he manages.

Max gets his card out of his bag and shows it to Ben: a drawing of Max standing and Ben sitting in his wheelchair next to an enormous cake with ten candles which he had run out of time to colour in. Inside it says, 'Happy Birthday from Max and Kew Class' and he has drawn some of his schoolmates – a diverse group of girls and boys. It is one of the loveliest cards I have ever seen.

When Max and Molly get fidgety I take them outside so they can run around. Molly is racing around on her scooter, trips and it falls into a pond. I rescue it and when she stops crying in shock we head in to recount the incident to Ben, scooter dripping on the café floor, and Ben giggles at our tale.

It is sometimes assumed that the relationships between our children are one-way – that Ben is the grateful recipient of Max and Molly's attention and affection, but it isn't true. Ben does love having his brother and sister around – he finds them funny and entertaining and cries when they are upset – but like all siblings, the dynamic is reciprocal. They can all wind each other up. Ben gets annoyed that Max is too noisy and Molly is climbing on him. Molly gets cross that Ben has pinched her arm and Max sometimes resents Ben not wanting to watch a particular programme. But when Max went to a play scheme at Ben's school he asked if he could be in the same group as Ben so he felt less nervous. As I walked them into the school building, Max held onto the arm of Ben's wheelchair and when I left them in the classroom he was holding Ben's hand. When I went away for a week and spoke to James on the phone he said, 'Molly has been talking about how much she misses you but she says she is OK because she has her lovely brother Ben with her.' Max and Molly get to play with Ben's toys, live in a house with a lift, jump queues at museums and also be comforted and loved by their brother.

By the time we get home on Ben's birthday it's past the kids' dinner time. We have a hectic few hours feeding each child, getting Ben changed into pyjamas and his home chair, preparing his medications and brushing teeth. Molly is indignant when it is bedtime and has a meltdown. I have to tell Max six times to put his pyjamas on and the laundry basket is so full it's in danger of occupying the whole room. That night, James starts reading Ben the fourth illustrated Harry Potter book which we have given him that morning. We have been buying him one a year for the last four years and we've now reached *The Goblet of Fire*. I pop in just before James finishes to kiss Ben goodnight under the fragmented light of his disco ball. It's been ten years of Ben and so much has happened. It's been ten years of wonder.

I have learned what can happen if you fall in love with a man who won't falter when tested, how much it is possible to love your own children, what comes of determination and stoicism, and really what is important. I've realized I can do hard things. We have weathered some storms and we're ready for the next ten years. I am so lucky to have three brilliant children who have taught me so much. No one wants to experience an earthquake but once the dust has settled, I see the cracks have let the light in.

BIBLIOGRAPHY

Books that I have read to Ben

A Light in the Attic, Shel Silverstein, London: Particular Books, 2011

Avocado Baby, John Burningham, London: Red Fox, 1994

Dear Zoo, Rod Campbell, London: Macmillan Children's Books, 2010

Goodnight Moon, Margaret Wise Brown & Clement Hurd, London: Macmillan's Children's Books, 2010

George's Marvellous Medicine, Roald Dahl & Quentin Blake, London: Puffin, 2010

Green Eggs and Ham, Dr. Seuss, London: HarperCollins, 2003

Harry Hill's Whopping Great Joke Book, Harry Hill, London: Faber & Faber, 2008

Harry Potter and the Goblet of Fire, J. K. Rowling & Jim Kay, London: Bloomsbury, 2019

Harry Potter and the Philosopher's Stone, J. K. Rowling & Jim Kay, London: Bloomsbury, 2015

Iggy Peck Architect, Andrea Beaty & David Roberts, New York: Abrams Books for Young Readers, 2007

Just William: Volume 2, Richmal Crompton, narrated by Martin Jarvis, London: BBC Physical Audio, 2003

Little Rabbit Foo Foo, Michael Rosen & Arthur Robins, London: Walker Books, 2003

Michael Rosen's Big Book of Bad Things, Michael Rosen, London: Puffin, 2010

Not Now, Bernard, David McKee, London: Andersen Press, 1980

Poo Bum, Stephanie Blake, Wellington: Gecko Press, 2013

Prince Dandypants and the Masked Avenger, Kaye Umansky, narrated by Robert Llewellyn, Audible Studios, 2016

Shark in the Park!, Nick Sharratt, London: Corgi, 2007

Stick Man, Julia Donaldson & Axel Scheffler, London: Alison Green Books, 2010

That's Not My Car, Fiona Watt & Rachel Wells, London: Usborne, 2004

The Bookshop Girl, Sylvia Bishop & Ashley King, London: Scholastic, 2017

The Ghost of Grania O'Malley, Michael Morpurgo, London: Egmont, 2013

The Magic Faraway Tree, Enid Blyton, London: Egmont, 2014

The Twits, Roald Dahl & Quentin Blake, London: Puffin, 2010

The Very Hungry Caterpillar, Eric Carle, London: Puffin, 1994

The Wheels on the Bus, David Ellwand, Bicester: Baker & Taylor, 2010

Other books mentioned in the text

Life After Birth, Kate Figes, London: Virago, 2008

The Mother of All Questions, Rebecca Solnit, London: Granta Books, 2017

Tonia Christie blog: https://www.ellenstumbo.com/growing-up-with-a-disability-the-preschool-years/

FURTHER READING

For younger kids

A Kids Book About Disabilities, Kristine Napper, A Kids Book About, 2020

Don't Call Me Special: A First Look at Disability, Pat Thomas & Lesley Harker, Hachette Children's Group, 2010

Hiya Moriah, Victoria Nelson & Boddz, Virginia Beach: Köehler Kids, 2019

I Am Not a Label, Cerrie Burnell & Lauren Baldo, London: Quarto Publishing, 2020

I Love You Natty, Mia Goleniowska & Hayley Goleniowska, Downs Side Up, 2014

I'm Special, Jen Green & Mike Gordon, London: Wayland Publishers, 1999

It's Okay to be Different, Todd Parr, New York: Little, Brown Young Readers, 2009

Little People, Big Dreams: Stephen Hawking, Isabel Sanchez Vegara & Matt Hunt, London: Frances Lincoln Children's Books, 2019

Mama Zooms, Jane Cowen-Fletcher, London: Scholastic, 1993

Max the Champion, Sean Stockdale, Alex Strick & Ros Asquith, London: Frances Lincoln Children's Books, 2014

Mermaid, Cerrie Burnell & Laura Ellen Anderson, London: Scholastic, 2015

My Friend Suhana: A Story of Friendship and Cerebral Palsy, Shaila Abdullah & Aanyah Abdullah, Ann Arbor: Loving Healing Press, 2014

Not So Different: What You Really Want to Ask About Having a Disability, Shane Burcaw, New York: Roaring Brook Press, 2017

Simply Mae, Kyle Fiorelli & Kellen Roggenbuck, KR Publishing, 2019

Susan Laughs, Jeanne Willis & Tony Ross, London: Andersen Press, 2011

The Abilities In Me: Tube Feeding, Gemma Keir & Adam Walker-Parker, The Abilities In Me, 2020

The Adventures of Team Super Tubie, Kristin Meyer & Kevin Cannon, Saint Paul: Beaver's Pond Press, 2017

The Boy Who Grew Flowers, Jen Wojtowicz & Steve Adams, Cambridge: Barefoot Books, 2012

The Five of Us, Quentin Blake, London: Tate Publishing, 2014

The Girl Who Thought in Pictures: The Story of Dr Temple Grandin, Julia Finley Mosca & Daniel Rieley, Seattle: The Innovation Press, 2017

Through the Eyes of Me, Jon Roberts & Hannah Rounding, Llanelli: Graffeg, 2017

We're All Wonders, R. J. Palacio, London: Puffin, 2017

We'll Paint the Octopus Red, Stephanie Stuve-Bodeen & Pam DeVito, Bethesda: Woodbine House, 1998

When Charley Met Emma, Amy Webb & Merrilee Liddiard, Minneapolis: Beaming Books, 2019

www.scope.org.uk/advice-and-support/storybooks-featuring-disabled-children/

For older kids

Department of Ability comic, available from www.departmentofability.com

Truth or Dare, Non Pratt, London: Walker Books, 2017

Wonder, R. J. Palacio, London: Corgi Books, 2014

For insights on parenting, disability and inclusion

Constellations: Reflections from Life, Sinéad Gleeson, London: Picador, 2019

Dear Parents…, Micheline Mason, Nottingham: Inclusive Solutions, 2008

Disability Visibility: First-Person Stories from the Twenty-First Century, ed. Alice Wong, New York: Vintage Books, 2020

Eye Can Write: A Memoir of a Child's Silent Soul, Jonathan Bryan, London: Lagom, 2018

Far From the Tree: Parents, Children and the Search for Identity, Andrew Solomon, London: Vintage, 2014

Four Fingers and Thirteen Toes, Rosaleen Moriarty-Simmonds, Milton Keynes: AuthorHouse, 2009

Letter to Louis, Alison White, London: Faber & Faber, 2018

My Left Foot, Christy Brown, London: Vintage, 1990

Say Hello, Carly Findlay, Sydney: HarperCollins, 2019

Sitting Pretty: The View from My Ordinary Resilient Disabled Body, Rebekah Taussig, New York: HarperOne, 2020

Strangers Assume My Girlfriend Is My Nurse, Shane Burcaw, New York: Roaring Brook Press, 2019

Tender: The Imperfect Art of Caring, Penny Wincer, London: Coronet, 2020

The Pretty One: On Life, Pop Culture, Disability and Other Reasons to Fall in Love with Me, Keah Brown, New York, Atria, 2019

The Reason I Jump: One Boy's Voice from the Silence of Autism, Naoki Higashida, London: Sceptre, 2013

The World I Fell Out Of, Melanie Reid, London: 4th Estate, 2019

*What the **** is Normal?!*, Francesca Martinez, London: Virgin Books, 2014

Charities and Awareness Groups

Contact A Family – For Families with Disabled Children
https://contact.org.uk

Council for Disabled Children
https://councilfordisabledchildren.org.uk/resources-and-help/im-parent

Disability Rights UK
https://www.disabilityrightsuk.org

Inclusion London – Directory of Deaf and Disabled People's Organisations https://www.inclusionlondon.org.uk/directory/listing/

Scope – Disability Equality Charity
https://www.scope.org.uk

ACKNOWLEDGEMENTS

So many people have helped and encouraged me to write this book, either by hearing early pieces and bolstering my confidence, or by giving me valuable feedback on later drafts. Particular thanks to Julie Garton, Irene Lomas and fellow students at Morley College; Rebecca Schiller and fellow writers at her Mothers Who Write retreat; Sarah Butler, Buffy Price, Alex Patrick and Cornelia Broesskamp.

There would be no book without the enthusiasm of my agent Cathryn Summerhayes, and the expertise of the accomplished people at Octopus Books: my brilliant, supportive editor Claudia Connal, Emily Brickell, Ella Parsons, Jaz Bahra, Megan Brown, Victoria Scales and others who have helped the book along. I have loved everything about the process of writing a book and it is all the better for having been a team effort. Thank you all.

My family wouldn't have got this far without Russell Levy and his team always having our backs.

I wouldn't have got anything done without all of the people (mostly women) who have looked after my children. Thank you to all the carers, teachers, assistants, therapists, doctors, nurses, advocates and allies who have supported us all, particularly Ben.

Thank you to the friends and acquaintances who have read Ben stories, made us all laugh, offered us tissues and picked up the things, actual and metaphorical, that we have dropped along the way.

Thank you to my family – by birth and marriage – who have always supported me, offered unconditional love to my children, and put in hours and hours of childcare: Mum, Dad, Maddy, Rosie, George, Prudence, Paul and Harry.

Lastly, James who is the love of my life, my best friend and my biggest fan. Apologies if I have made it seem like you were always away. Actually you are the backbone of our family. I will always feel lucky that I met you and that we made these precious children.

ABOUT THE AUTHOR

Jessica Moxham's eldest son, Ben, is disabled, uses a wheelchair and needs assistance to communicate. Jessica's writing discusses how she and her family support him with – and learn from – his disability. Her work is read by parents, health professionals and educators, among others.

Jessica has given lectures to health professionals on her family's experience, from small groups of students to larger audiences at the Royal College of Paediatrics and Child Health. She has been interviewed on BBC Radio 5 Live and has written for the *Guardian* on austerity and disability.

Jessica is also a qualified architect and has worked in London and the Middle East. She now lives in London with her husband and three children, in the house she redesigned to suit Ben.

Find Jessica's blog at son-stories.com or follow her on Instagram and Twitter at @jessmoxham.